Changing Minds

Changing Minds

A Guide to Facilitated Participatory Planning

Cole P. Dodge
Gavin Bennett

ACADEMIC FOUNDATION
NEW DELHI

International Development Research Centre
Ottawa • Cairo • Dakar • Montevideo • Nairobi • New Delhi • Singapore

First published in 2011
by

ACADEMIC FOUNDATION
4772-73 / 23 Bharat Ram Road, (23 Ansari Road),
Darya Ganj, New Delhi - 110 002 (India).
Phones : 23245001 / 02 / 03 / 04.
Fax : +91-11-23245005.
E-mail : books@academicfoundation.com
www. academicfoundation.com

and

INTERNATIONAL DEVELOPMENT RESEARCH CENTRE
PO Box 8500, Ottawa, ON, K1G 3H9
Canada
E-mail: info@idrc.ca
www.idrc.ca

This work was carried out with the aid of a grant from the Wellcome Trust, London, UK, Canada's International Development Research Centre (IDRC), and the UK Government's Department for International Development. The views expressed herein do not necessarily represent those of IDRC, the Wellcome Trust, or the Department for International Development.

Cataloging in Publication Data--DK
Courtesy: D.K. Agencies (P) Ltd. <docinfo@dkagencies.com>

Dodge, Cole P.
Changing minds : a guide to facilitated participatory planning/
Cole P. Dodge, Gavin Bennett.
p. cm.
Includes bibliographical references (p.).
ISBN 9788171888603
ISBN (e-book) 9781552504932

1. Participatory rural appraisal--Developing countries. 2. Participatory rural appraisal--Africa. 3. Infrastructure (Economics)--Developing countries. 4. Infrastructure (Economics)--Africa. 5. Participatory rural appraisal--Developing countries--Case studies. 6. Participatory rural appraisal--Africa--Case studies. I. Bennett, Gavin, joint author. II. Title.

DDC 307.1412091724 22

Typeset by Italics India, New Delhi.
Printed and bound in India.

Contents

Section C
TECHNIQUES

Section E
DELVING DEEPER

Foreword

I have been a participant in several major and successful processes using the techniques described in this book, and also in many planning exercises which followed a traditional, hierarchical approach.

While both approaches have their strengths and weaknesses, it is my view that in complex situations, as is the case with academic institutions, the Facilitated Participatory Planning (FPP) technique has the greater chance of success—of evoking ownership and bringing effective and lasting change. This view is based on personal involvement in three of the planning processes described here.

At Makerere University, I was the Dean of the Faculty of Medicine and we had failed, twice, through traditional planning processes to establish a College of Health Sciences. After meeting with the facilitator, Cole P. Dodge, to chart a course for the participatory planning process, I was at once both stimulated and skeptical. Skeptical because only one-third of the planning committee would be drawn from the Faculty of Medicine while two-thirds were from the wider stakeholders, including government ministries, professional associations, non-governmental service providers and Makerere University Council. I feared they would not necessarily have the welfare of "my" Faculty at heart.

Facilitated Participatory Planning for the College took a year. It was a resounding success.

Such were the intrinsic strengths of the process, that when IDRC approved a grant involving FPP across the three countries of the East African Community (Uganda, Kenya and Tanzania) to establish an evidence-based policy initiative, I was confident that it could be done.

Later, the planning for the James P. Grant School of Public Health within BRAC University in Bangladesh was dovetailed into the global Health Human Resource Commission and brought together a dozen of the best schools of public health in the world—along with policy makers, academics and leaders. Using FPP, a consensus was reached and the new school was launched in 2004.

It was especially interesting to see the progression of FPP—starting with Makerere, extending to the East African region, and then involving an international group from two dozen countries which required partnership between universities in the North and a new private university in the South.

The purpose of this book—which is instructed by that progression—is to promote FPP in the context of complex institutions. A first book was published by Makerere Institute of Social Research in 2002 to encourage participatory facilitation within Uganda. This updated and expanded work has a wider audience in mind.

Building institutional capacity in Africa is severely afflicted by implementation, resource mobilisation, sustainability and management difficulties. These problems must be overcome if Africa is to meet the complex challenges of disease, health care service delivery, low capacity for research, and the need for modern academic programmes (amid emerging technologies) within the context of chronic poverty and underdevelopment. Frequently, these problems begin with inadequate planning processes. FPP is thus a pivotal part of the solution—it lends itself easily to planning for enhanced institutional capacities, either through transformation of existing institutions or by creating new ones.

For academics, researchers and managers who require a planning process which goes beyond the hierarchical approach, the wealth of detail and description here will give them the confidence to consider FPP. For professionals who want to become skilled facilitators of planning, this book forms the basis of an intensive training programme.

I wholeheartedly recommend Facilitated Participatory Planning, based on my first-hand experience of the successes which have been and can be achieved.

— Professor Nelson Sewankambo

Principal,
College of Health Sciences,
Makerere University

Authors' note

Planning...
Planning for change...
Changing the way change is planned...

In Uganda, a military junta and years of civil war crippled the country and collapsed most of its institutions in it. All have since been repaired and revived, but many are still not fit for purpose...because while they were in limbo the world moved on, in technology, in scale, in social patterns and priorities. These institutions had to be fundamentally redesigned. But how? By whom?

In Bangladesh, BRAC University—which was established and staff-led on an international "ivy league" model—wanted more home-grown design and relevance in its new School of Public Health. How could North and South first plan together and then work together to make the concept a win-win for both styles?

In East Africa, the countries of Kenya, Tanzania and Uganda have borders and much else in common with each other, from language and culture to poverty and health problems. Yet each member of this natural regional bloc ploughs a lonely furrow through its own harsh socio-economic landscape. All know what benefits synergy could bring, but how do they even start to turn historic hurdles into modern bridges?

In Kenya alone, traditional divisions have led to chronic politicisation of everything, so status and patronage are often much more influential than merit or performance. In this situation, how can relatively abundant but piecemeal resources for health research work cohesively at a truly national level? What objective plan can depolarise the politics and sustainably bypass them?

Such are the intractable issues that Facilitated Participatory Planning (FPP) is equipped to address (see Chapter 3).

These are just some of the cases that have highlighted the need for, and contributed wisdom to, development of the FPP process and the publication of this book.

Preface

Throughout middle Africa, there is a supposition that infrastructure and essential services are inefficient because they do not have enough money. However, an equal truth is that they do not have enough money because they are inefficient.

Certainly, resources are limited. Most developing countries have per capita GDPs of less than $1,000 per year (industrialised countries are at least 20 times more affluent).

OVER A BARREL...

The South not only needs to increase its means, but also mend its ways

The 90/10 divide is a reality—some 90 per cent of resources are in the North to address 10 per cent of the world's public health problems, leaving the South with 10 per cent of global resources to face 90 per cent of the disease burden.

Certainly capacity must be developed to manage this disparity, and increased service capacity requires more skills, more equipment, more materials...and all of those take hard cash.

But in a great many cases, the first and bigger problem is that the modest resources that are available are not used to best effect; the systems are often so sub-optimal that even if more resources were heaped upon them, they would still not deliver with significantly greater impact.

Throughout the world there is increasing awareness and focus that, in parallel with resource support, there needs to be systems change—a profound transformation—to make better use of existing resources as well as building capacity to attract and apply more.

There are no silver bullets in this process. National and institutional infrastructures are highly complex; trans-sectoral, multi-disciplinary, multi-departmental, each with its own unique personality, context and issues.

But there is one golden rule. If they are to work well, the systems must be designed by the people who run them and the people who use them—the front line stakeholders.

The remedies must be tailored. Case-by-case. But just as importantly, the method of designing the remedies—the transformations—must be flexible, too. It must be able to "fit" each specific institution, uniquely and exactly.

So the first challenge, then, is not to transform middle Africa's institutions. It is to transform the way the change is planned! That is what FPP enables and then steers.

Acknowledgements

Canada's International Development Research Centre (IDRC), the Swiss Agency for Development and Cooperation (SDC), UK's Department for International Development (DFID), the Wellcome Trust, the Bangladesh Rural Advancement Committee (BRAC), and the Rockefeller Foundation are recognised for their support of FPP in the development and transformation of institutions. The following institutions have engaged the processes from which the materials presented in this book evolved:

2000	Makerere Institute of Social Research (Uganda).
2001	Innovations at Makerere Committee (I@mak.com).
2004	James P. Grant School of Public Health, BRAC University (Bangladesh).
2006	REACH-Policy Initiative, East African Community.
2007	Health Research Capacity Strengthening Initiative (Kenya).
2008	Comprehensive Planning Committee, Makerere College of Health Sciences.

Other organisations which have used this facilitation approach include World Bank Millennium Science Initiative, African Psychiatric Association, UNICEF, World Food Programme, UNDP, Femnet, Action Aid, FIDA, Care International, African Economic Research Consortium, Rockefeller Foundation, Canada's International Development Research Centre, Fredrick Ebert Foundation, Norwegian Church Aid, and Swedish Save the Children Fund.

Individuals who contributed to these developments include Neil Mckee, chief architect of Visualization in Participatory Programs; Profs. PJM Ssebuwufu and Livingstone S. Luboobi, Vice Chancellors of Makerere University who welcomed facilitation into the University community; Prof. Nelson Sewankambo, Principal, College of Health Sciences, Makerere University; Graham Reid and Nasreen Jessani, IDRC; Don de Savigny, Swiss Tropical Institute; Dr. Hassan Mshinda, former Director of Ifakara Health Institute, Tanzania, and now Director General of the Tanzanian Commission for Science and Technology, Cheikh Mbacke and Joyce Moock, formerly at Rockefeller Foundation; and Michael Crawford at the World Bank.

Individuals who have championed the FPP process, and the hierarchies who have listened to them, are to be commended.

This work was carried out with the aid of a grant from the Wellcome Trust, London, UK; the International Development Research Centre, Ottawa, Canada; and the UK Government's Department for International Development. The views expressed herein do not necessarily represent those of IDRC, the Wellcome Trust or the Department for International Development.

Section A

INTRODUCTION

1 Planning methods

FPP does not change the basic principles or framework of what a plan is. It changes the way that plan is made.

The need to change

Evolution or revolution?

All institutions are constantly faced with the need to change—to allow growth, to technically upgrade, to meet new market demands or socio-economic needs.

This change can be achieved through progressive evolution...in most areas...for some time. But eventually, and especially if there is a dramatic shift in size, technology or circumstances, more fundamental transformation is necessary. A revolution! The original set-up, even if admired and successful, can no longer cope with demand or can no longer deliver to the required scope, scale and standard. (Such conditions are now chronic in higher education in middle Africa—see Mamdani, 2007)

Once this change moment has moved from advisable to unavoidable (deferring upheaval is a universal tendency), the necessary design surgery is traditionally conducted by the incumbent hierarchy or it is delegated to independent consultants.

The way to change

The big difference

The world of "planning" is awash with different models and techniques. But whatever they are called, whoever they involve and however they are conducted, all essentially do some version of SWOT (Strengths, Weaknesses, Opportunities, Threats) analysis, all identify objectives, and all decide what change must be made, who will do what, make a list of needs, declare result-orientated targets, define how outcomes will be measured, and set cost and time boundaries.

Facilitated Participatory Planning (FPP) does not change these principles, and indeed the plan that it produces has a completely recognisable framework. What FPP does change, fundamentally, is *how* the plan is made. That may seem like a small difference. Perhaps. But it is an all-important one. For the process of making a plan can dramatically change the insight and accuracy of the SWOT analysis, the practicality of the target results, the acceptability of the methods, and hence the probability of successful implementation.

THE PERFECT SOLUTION?

Outsiders can bring both technical expertise...and practical insights

What FPP does, above all, is ensure that people directly affected by the plan and those who will implement it also participate in its formulation. Indeed, *they make the plan*.

If the plan-making process is conducted by a single individual, or by one unit among many, it is by definition a unilateral perspective. So, too, if it is made by a hierarchy, where status can outweigh or intimidate alternative voices. Such a plan will be limited to that individual's or that unit's or that superior's ideas and view. It will contain potential conflicts with other stakeholders which may not even have been identified, never mind resolved. It will overlook at least some crucial issues which the makers of the plan were not aware of. While it may offer remedies to some problems, undoubtedly it will *cause* others.

HIERARCHICAL PLANNING
The closed loop

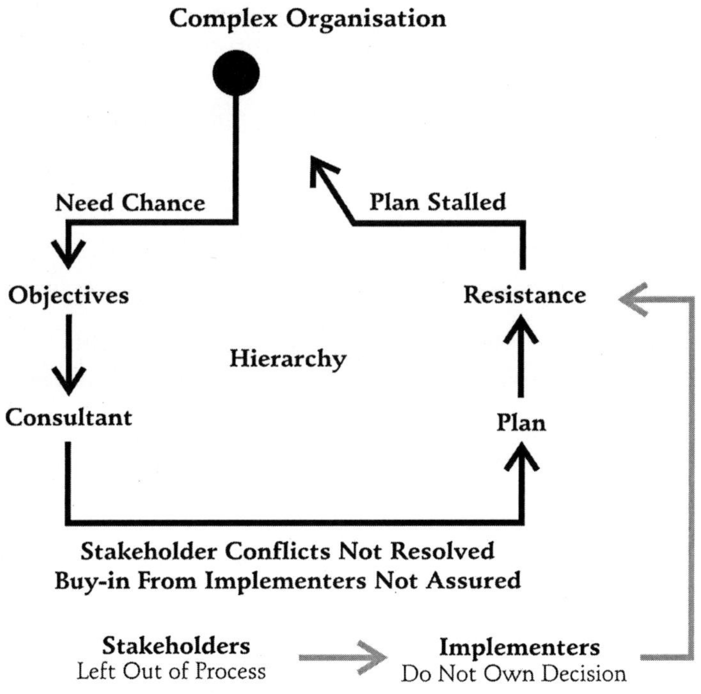

Even if that unilateral plan is presented for group discussion, it will be a finished product, not a blue-sky or blank-page that is being offered to wider opinion. In a usually brief "speak now or forever hold your peace" review, even the most radical critics will be able to do little more than panel beat the traditional, and often old, programme vehicle.

The "own-do" gap

What doesn't work

Too often, donors support planning processes which fail to adequately involve the people who will be charged with implementation, leading to an "own-do" gap. Similarly, planning processes in developing countries routinely follow traditional hierarchical approaches which fail to generate or allow innovation and models promoting "change". They therefore fall short in either the transformation of established institutions or creation of dynamic capacities in research, learning and management.

Most crucially, in either the hierarchical or consultancy method, the plan is not made by—and does not belong to—those who will implement and live with it. However expert or "correct" the authors believe the plan to be, other stakeholders have no sense of ownership and are thus less likely to be supportive...and might even actively oppose the plan.

A plan made by FPP does not seek bolt-on group opinion on a finished product. It seeks built-in stakeholder opinion from the start—and throughout. Stakeholders are not merely involved in the process—they *make* the plan themselves.

By the time the completed plan emerges, potential conflicts have been identified and discussed and resolved, drawing on a wide spectrum of opinion and containing all dimensions of existing knowledge. The plan is already the thoroughly deliberated, carefully considered, fully agreed view. Individuals within the group have not grudgingly compromised their personal preferences—they have understood what will work best for everybody. The plan is not unilaterally composed or imposed. It is devised and owned—mutually—by all concerned.

PARTICIPATORY PLANNING

The inclusive process

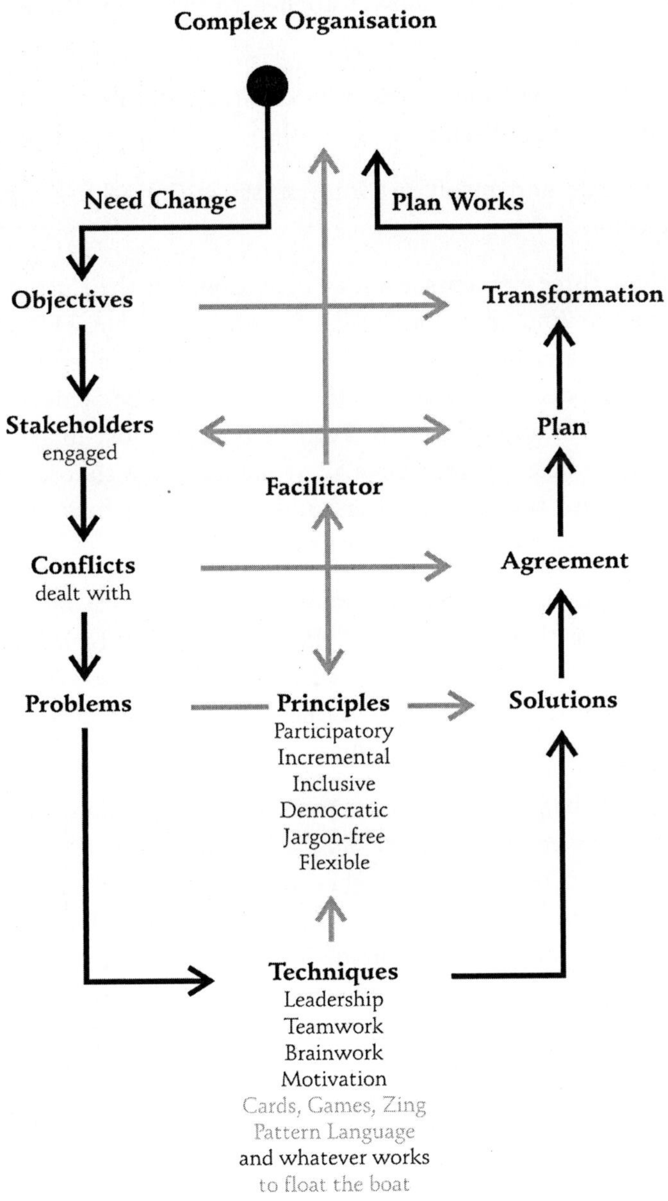

FPP is not simplistic—it is a sophisticated technique and an always dynamic process—but it does simplify the planning task with three distinctive features:

- It amplifies the brainpower applied to planning (by involving all stakeholders).
- It gets the best out of them by engaging a professional facilitator (external specialist); and
- It reveals and resolves complex issues (by asking incremental questions).

None of these three elements is a new invention, but their use in effective combination is. And that combination—which is what FPP is—can be used to address any planning or other management challenge. Whatever the planning model, and whatever the quest, it can be achieved through FPP better than in any other way. For FPP does not just make a plan; or perhaps an even better plan. Above all, it makes a plan that is more likely to work—because the implementers understand what has been decided and believe in both the aims and the design.

The old methods use hierarchical insiders and technical outsiders. The option to reverse that—to give the planning baton to technical insiders with an external facilitator and no pecking order—has always existed, but for obvious reasons has been resisted (hierarchies tend to prefer hierarchy) and has lacked professional technique.

Two things are changing that reflex: the degree, speed and scale of change has exposed the weaknesses of the old practice, and there are now refined, tested and proven techniques for FPP—drawing input horizontally from right across the institution and all its disciplines, and at the same time gaining the understanding, the pre-disposed support and the unanimous agreement (not just an emasculated consensus) of those who will actually implement and live the new set-up.

The evidence is stark: Redesign by incumbent hierarchies and external consultancies usually does not work. Redesign by FPP often does.

This book

Design and objective

The purpose of this book is to answer the most crucial questions about FPP:

What is it?

Why use it?

How is it done?

Whoever you are—whether you are a potential customer, or a potential practitioner, a policy maker, a regulator, or a professional working in an institutional context—and whatever your interest or objectives, these pages will lift FPP from something you have "heard about" to something you "thoroughly understand".

You will know what the choices are, what the process is, the skills that are needed, the resources and challenges that are involved, and the key principles which are essential to success.

That is all this book does. But it does all that.

2 Overview

What is FPP?

> If you ask the wrong question, there can be no such thing as a right answer. Get the question right and the answer is often obvious…
>
> Above all, FPP asks the right questions—one at a time.

Definition

Participatory Planning (PP) is a system in which all stakeholders come together to brainstorm ideas which are progressively consolidated into a plan. Facilitated Participatory Planning (FPP) engages an outside specialist to enable the stakeholders to maximise *their* performance and optimise *their* result.

Although "incremental questions" may be categorised as a process, they are so central and fundamental to the FPP system itself, they must form part of its definition.

Process

In practice, an independent Board is appointed to select a group of stakeholders (the Task Force) to represent a full cross-section of interests and disciplines. The Task Force is fully empowered, and then brainstorms at a series of "retreats", usually run over several months.

Each retreat typically lasts two or three days. Each day is divided into sessions, allocated to plenary or group work. There may also be external visits and meetings between retreats.

The conduct of retreats/days/sessions is crucial, using varied techniques and sophisticated reflexes to—progressively—homogenise diverse interests and characters, relax tensions, build teamwork, inspire interest, expunge jargon, draw out ideas, and get to core issues...primarily through step-by-step questions. Input is based on "every voice counts". The discussion of ideas and the making of a plan are concurrent.

Questions lead the process. The reasons and techniques are fully elaborated in Chapter 6.

> Questions are used to gather facts, to elicit opinions and to stimulate ideas. They validate FPP's claim to stakeholders that it is *your* voice that counts. They tell participants that this is a genuinely blue-sky approach, where the job is to identify problems and discover remedies afresh, without preconception or imposed statement. The system listens. The target is something new, something different—Change.
>
> Just as importantly, the questions must be incremental, allowing participants to examine and understand the issues brick by brick. A question that goes straight to a multi-faceted end-point will hit a wall of preconceptions, prejudices, blind spots, and entrenched vested interests. It will result in argumentative battle lines and a confusion of half-understood and misunderstood issues.
>
> With incremental questions each one is only a small component of the overall subject, so it is clearer, less complex, less threatening, and is more likely to receive open-minded and objective answers.
>
> By the time many answers to many questions build up into a global picture, the facts and practicalities (from all viewpoints) are known and thoroughly understood. Agreement between different vested interests is not only more possible; it is probable.

Empowerment

The plan assigns its own drivers but, on completion, a team (usually including key members of the Task Force) is put in place to defend the principles of the plan and ensure they are not hijacked by hierarchical manipulation or other vested-interest interference during implementation.

Enlightened leaders/managers opting for FPP need to buy into empowerment of the group and guarantee the integrity of the plan from the outset. That is fundamental to the group's confidence, commitment and real sense of ownership. That is what makes the process—and the plan—work.

Facilitation

There is no pecking order in the planning work. An external facilitator with group management and planning skills guides the process. The use of a facilitator neutralises conflicts in the group, promotes objectivity, maintains focus, and organises the process (brainstorming) and the product (a plan).

While the facilitator is necessarily an outsider—who brings consultancy-type skills—s/he does not make the plan. The stakeholders do, and for this reason the result is better-balanced and "owned" by the implementers, much improving the chances of its success.

The facilitator helps ensure the right questions are asked, and helps the participants liberate and marshal the answers. *Their* answers.

Further training

Most people require experience to become good facilitators and there can be no instant "teach yourself" manual which embraces all that is required to manage a participatory process. For those interested in becoming facilitators, this manual, even in its entirety, is written to be used with an intensive training course lasting a week or more (see Chapter 18).

Also, FPP itself has emerging technology—from flip charts to PowerPoint, from cards on pinboards to interactive computerised screens. More techniques, such as Pattern Language, are being explored. The process will be optimised if the leadership and the Task Force can be familiarised with the concepts of FPP in advance.

What is it for?

FPP for complex institutions grows directly out of the need to improve planning processes in situations which are entrenched or stagnated, highly competitive, or loaded with conflicts. It is based on participatory techniques designed to diffuse tensions, identify and tackle core problems, generate relevant solutions, enhance commitment and create a culture of effective teamwork. FPP refers to a creative combination of different approaches to planning, involving all stakeholders, centred around professional facilitation, and based on questions.

FPP has been applied in various group events such as planning for and implementation of institutional transformation, storyline development, project planning, business meetings, cultural orientation, team building, training of trainers, gender training, and dissemination of research findings, among other contexts.

"Changing Minds"—changing the way change is made using FPP—explores both the need and the method for a planning process which allows diverse perspectives to be considered and respected by colleagues and decision makers.

While this book is framed in the context of complex institutions, such as universities and academic or research bodies, clearly FPP can be effective in almost any situation—from rural communities to industrial federations, from national policies to international accords.

Who is it for?

The FPP process began to evolve an identity of its own about 20 years ago. It has since been tried, tested, proven and further refined. This book represents a state-of-the-art consolidation of the techniques developed and the wisdom gained in the first two decades.

It has two audiences in mind—**senior people** responsible for institutions, academic programmes or research; and the **facilitators** who lead and manage planning of programmes for creation of new institutions, institutional transformation, branding or evaluation of health, research or institutional planning processes.

In the complex institution context, the first audience is mostly civil servants (managers, administrators, policy makers and technical specialists); it includes academics, researchers, administrators and teaching staff of universities (vice chancellors, deans, directors, department heads, professors, lecturers as well as bursars, librarians, registrars and managers). It also includes anyone else who holds a leadership or management position within civil society, such as NGO leaders, managers and project implementers plus private sector service providers, pharmaceutical companies, community organisations, professional bodies as well as all donor organisations which support research or academic programmes (bilateral, multilateral, northern academic institutions working in partnership with southern institutions, foundations, contractors and sponsors of programmes).

The second audience is the planners, consultants and other professionals responsible for planning or planning functions. These include professional planners, within government or university structures, the facilitators/consultants who are contracted to assist with planning processes, as well as committee members with the mandate for institutional planning. All the chapters are significant for this second audience, and Sections B, C and D provide background and detail that will certainly reinforce and guide qualified facilitators in their work and give newcomers to the facilitation process a strong grounding.

3 Compelling evidence

Transformation at Makerere University in Uganda

Context

Makerere University, once pre-eminent in Africa and world-renowned, suffered stagnation, decline and neglect following Uganda's military coup in 1971, the ensuing 15 years of civil war, and a further decade of limbo as the National Resistance Movement tried to rebuild a broken country.

For perspective: academic salaries in US dollar terms fell by 90 per cent. There was zero growth in admissions and less than 10 per cent increase in graduates over a period of nearly 30 years. In the same period, the population of Uganda more than doubled from 9 million to 22 million people. The Ministry of Health's estimated doctor-population ratio in 1970 was 1:11,000. At the turn of the 21st century, the estimate was 1:22,000. In sum, after three decades a situation which was far from good had become twice as bad (Wiebe and Dodge, 1987).

In parallel, the disease burden soared—with the HIV/AIDS pandemic, the outbreak of ebola, and the resurgence of infectious and non-infectious diseases. Infant, under-five child and maternal mortality rates were among the highest in the world. Further, during reconstruction, state priorities focussed on universal primary education, which had greater social and economic benefits in terms of investment.

Thus, Makerere was dilapidated, under-funded and decades out-of-date technologically as the economy grew in the 1990s and families were able to afford—and demand—university education. So, too, young professionals basing their prospects on peace, stability and an expanding economy were eager to enrol in night classes.

To meet these demands; Makerere decided to admit private fee-paying students. While this led to an enrolment explosion from 3,000 in 1990 to more than 15,000 by 2002, it also wrought havoc with the structures, capacities and relationships of the University's faculties, departments and institutes.

Makerere recognised well enough that these and other factors required revolutionary transformation. Diligent and expert plans using traditional processes were formulated, but these made little progress—there was simply no buy-in among key stakeholders for programmes that were seen as unilaterally formulated and hierarchically imposed.

Enter FPP

The Makerere Institute of Social Research tried a different approach— at a four-day planning retreat for *all* of their staff. The Director was so impressed by the results that she became the advocate ("champion") and promoter of the participatory concept.

The Rockefeller Foundation subsequently tried a facilitated annual work planning retreat itself, and then funded a participatory planning initiative towards institutional transformation within Makerere University. FPP was subsequently undertaken in the following six processes:

1. I@mak.com, Innovation at Makerere Committee.
2. Maxplan.com, Makerere Committee for Planning Transformation of the Faculty of Medicine into a College of Health Sciences.
3. Pentaplan.com, Planning Committee for College of Humanities and Behavioural Sciences.
4. Plan-4-Five, Planning for a combined College of Agriculture and Veterinary Sciences.
5. Strategic Planning, for Makerere University.
6. Millennium Science Initiative.

Out of these six, three were funded by Rockefeller Foundation and others by Ford Foundation, Carnegie Corporation of New York and the World Bank (Dodge *et al.*, 2003).

Outcomes

All three driving forces of transformation were achieved:

- To make higher education more relevant to the country and society—there are now 22 academic units with an annual budget of $56 million, more than 40 per cent of students are females, and a vibrant research culture is giving the whole of Uganda the capacity for evidence-based decision-making.
- To improve the quality of undergraduate education to meet the evolving challenges of the 21st century—the university's ICT technology has been revolutionised, more than 8,000 open access journals are available, more staff have PhDs, some 6 per cent of students are international, units are writing competitive research proposals that win funding, lecturers are building research groups around themselves with increasingly sophisticated and funded laboratories and other facilities.
- To increase the number of students to meet current and future demand (and need) for university admissions and graduates—Makerere currently has an enrolment of 32,000. It produces 5,000 graduates per year.

Innovation at Makerere Committee was launched on plans generated by FPP. The task force comprised 50 per cent government officials and went on to secure the largest grant Makerere had ever received (World Bank and Rockefeller Foundation). Significantly, the response among academic staff at Makerere to the very idea of "participatory" planning was overwhelming, with 90 per cent attendance at launch of the innovations programme and a total of nearly 1,000 concept papers, proposals and projects subsequently emerging!

Also, all planning processes and the management of change within the University are now based on principles of participation, team building and involvement of stakeholders.

In sum, Makerere has undergone a transformation of such scale and vigour that it is studied and cited as an example by institutions such as the World Bank Institute, the African Studies Institute at Uppsala, and UNESCO.

Strengthening health research capacity in Kenya

Context

Kenya's population has nearly quintupled in less than half-a-century since independence to approximately 38 million,[1] with 10 per cent in the capital Nairobi, 10 per cent in other major urban centres, and 80 per cent (served by about 20 per cent of the health professionals) in rural areas.

Despite ethnic divisions, infrastructural shortfalls and numerous governance issues, Kenya has a multitude of research institutions, 12 public universities and 21 private universities,[2] their affiliated institutions, and a plethora of technical colleges, training institutes and polytechnics.

Health research at any of these comes under three—*all* ostensibly overarching—layers of drive and control: The Kenya Medical Research Institute (KEMRI) established in 1979, the National Health and Research Development Center (NHRDC) created in 1994 within the Ministry of Science and Technology, and the National Council for Science and Technology (NCST) which governs "all" research. However:

- The calibre of institutions and teams varies considerably.
- The majority of the large academic centres and health care institutions are in Nairobi, with some in Kisumu, Eldoret (West) and Kilifi (Coast).
- Each part works on independent niche goals, often with a mono-disciplinary approach and little or no exchange or collaboration.
- Much of the work is driven by independent or donor interests rather than national priorities.
- KEMRI's original mandate was for bio-medical research only.
- NHRDC is chronically under-funded and hence ineffective.

---

1. Kenya population 2008 estimate. *Wikipedia*. Accessed November 27, 2008.
2. Kenya universities. *Wikipedia*. Accessed November 27, 2008.

- Academic research in Kenya has been plagued by inadequate remuneration, sub-optimal institutional support and better career opportunities elsewhere.
- The cohort of skilled researchers who have not been brain-drained is ageing.
- Gender parity is on the mend, but with a minimum of only 1F/3M, and that only aspirational, Kenya remains a patriarchal society.

Enter FPP

In 2005, Kenya's Ministry of Health was exploring a Sector Wide Approach (SWAp), and a scoping and design mission on research support was funded by DFID and Wellcome Trust.

The resulting documents guided a DFID-WT funded Health Research Capacity Strengthening (HRCS) Initiative (Vaughn *et al.*, 2005) with four goals:

- **Harmony:** Improved regulation and co-ordination of the national research environment.
- **Capacity:** Enhanced institutional capacity for high-quality, multi-disciplinary health-related research studies.
- **Synergy:** Scientific knowledge more effectively shared across international organisations and knowledge networks.
- **Policy:** National health policies and programmes formulated utilising research findings.

The special experience of Canada's IDRC was engaged for the planning process and a nationally led, participatory, multi-disciplinary local Task Force (TF) was formed to develop a long-term (20 years) vision and a short-term (5 years) strategic and operational plan.

Outcomes

The TF met eight times, at approximately three-week intervals, for two and-a-half days per session—Thursday 7pm to Saturday 5pm—at a "retreat" location.

The resulting proposal for a country-owned, country-led HRCS Initiative adhering to the four goals led to the formation of a new independent NGO called the Consortium for National Health Research (CNHR) and set out the structural, legal and operational framework for:

- Fully co-ordinating health research policy and regulation, nationally.
- Nurturing centres of excellence through training, career development awards, and competitive grant systems.
- Creating a knowledge repository to enable sharing of research findings and translation for non-technical users.
- Winning international funding support through proven performance.

These plans are now being implemented through funding from DFID-WT-IDRC for £10 million over five years with the intention of devolution and self-sustainability thereafter.

TF members found the process itself an inspiration. Their verdict: the new way of planning introduced a new way of thinking, their networks were expanded, relations were strengthened, their capacity was enhanced, and they felt a heightened sense of pride and empowerment as citizens with a role to play in the health of their nation (Jessani, unpublished).

Bridging the know-do gap in East Africa

Context

Kenya, Tanzania, and Uganda have stressed economies and exploding populations. They each suffer exceptionally high levels of preventable disease—HIV/AIDS, pneumonia, measles, and tuberculosis.

Individually, a root cause is inadequate knowledge and resources, and the prescribed cure is more money; though in all three cases the funding shortfalls are exacerbated by unnecessarily inefficient health delivery systems.

But another factor should not be underestimated: officials lack the information on which to make sound policy decisions. Either the right research is not conducted, or policy makers fail to hear or to heed good scientific advice. In either case, there is a yawning "know-do" gap.

In addressing this issue country by country, another anomaly emerges. Why do three countries, which once were and still could be a natural regional bloc, with so many geographic, climatic, demographic, cultural, social, and economic overlaps—and such very similar health issues—not collaborate? Without adding one cent of resource to any of their research programmes, this measure alone could treble the data available to all of them!

So in parallel with bringing researchers and policy makers together in a push-pull team effort, it made obvious sense to combine that effort—in Kenya, and in Tanzania and in Uganda—into a regional initiative.

Enter FPP

There was not just one challenge here but three times three. First, to get the know-do gap recognised as a core problem; second, to get researchers and policy makers round the same table; third, to get them to agree how to co-operate in one country. Then another. And another. And then together.

But the very essence of FPP is to take one step at a time, to progressively resolve differences and reach agreement so, by the time the big picture emerges from all the parts, there is already understanding, trust, teamwork and accord. So when Canada's International Development Research Centre (IDRC) proposed participatory planning between researchers and decision-makers in one country, it was the start of just one process that all stakeholders would ultimately take to a mutually devised and agreed final outcome.

Outcomes

The outcome was a plan to establish a new body called the Regional East African Community Health-Policy Initiative (REACH-Policy Initiative). It has been reviewed and endorsed by the East African Community as a political commitment.

REACH is intended to function as an independent bridge between researchers and policy makers, turning policy needs into scientific questions for researchers, and delivering the answers in terms that officials can work with. REACH will be the world's first regional experiment in knowledge translation using knowledge brokers.

REACH is expected to: host safe-harbour consultations between researchers and policy makers and other stakeholders; be a rapid response reference centre for data search; synthesise high priority information to order; deliver complex information in user-friendly packages; identify and fill research and policy gaps; and train both policy makers and researchers in knowledge translation.

REACH is designed to be an autonomous regional mediator, with "country nodes" to translate the research needs of each country's ministries, parliament and civil society into questions that the secretariat can investigate. These same offices should help convert answers into practical policy recommendations, and be proactive as well as reactive.

REACH's activities are likely to evolve step-by-step over the first five years as it instals the structures and processes required for a comprehensive knowledge translation system.

For more information about the implementation schedule and other details about the operation of the REACH-Policy Initiative, please see the full text of its prospectus (EAC, 2006).

Innovating public health training in Bangladesh

Context

Bangladesh's higher education system welcomes and needs foreign resources, but it subjects them to restrictive national concepts and regulations which are not always compatible with modern and flexible international thinking.

When Ford Foundation's seed grant established BRAC University as the country's first private university, planned on a liberal arts model by eminent academics from Harvard, Swarthmore and Brown, Bangladesh swiftly superimposed its own structures and curricula.

So when the university founded the James P. Grant School of Public Health, it was at once a dream come true and a nightmare: how to deliver the best international science and practice in a system which refuses reform, resists change and proscribes innovation; how to secure the commitment of lecturers from the world's best schools in such a context; and who would devise the curriculum to meet both state-of-the-art international standards and Bangladesh's national imperatives?

Experience with BRAC University itself showed that engaging a design consultant from the North would be futile; and while an internal planning team would satisfy the all-governing Bangladesh University Grants Commission and Ministries of Health and Education, their template could alienate the crucial support of world class academic staff.

Enter FPP

BRAC was already addressing the university's wider clash of concepts through a participatory experiment called "Initiative for Learning and Development", so FPP was the natural (and perhaps only) option for the School of Public Health.

The local and international positions were so polarised that the FPP process—even though rationalised to a planning team of just two local and two international public health officials—was stormy and seemingly intractable.

The facilitator tried all manner of FPP techniques, and one—field and comparator visits—finally worked. The FPP team visited seven schools of public health in the North and seven major stakeholders in Bangladesh, and formulated a plan based on discussion with the heads of those 14 institutions.

All 14 were then invited to a sounding board meeting in Dhaka to review whether the plan was worth testing.

Outcomes

The verdict was an instantaneous and unanimous vote for immediate implementation. Less than one hour later, the BRAC University Governing Board Chairman gave the go-ahead for working groups to draft the actual course content for the MPH within the modular plan.

The BRAC University School of Public Health has since produced five batches of graduates, and is cited by the World Health Organization (WHO) as one of the most innovative MPH programmes in the world (Chowdhury, 2007). In 2010 an international external evaluation of the school noted its curriculum, providing field exposure in virtually every course and high-quality teaching evidenced in the competencies of graduates, but the sustainability of JPGSPH is vitally dependent upon both funding and on recruiting and supporting a local faculty.

And more...

While FPP is designed for and best used in the "no shortcuts" context of full planning programmes, its principles and techniques are adaptable to many (almost any!) other situations.
For example...

Context

A Ministry of Health felt overwhelmed by a powerfully organised, donor-driven set of priorities, strategies, budgets and five-year-plan demands—but struggled to muster a cohesive position of its own to balance the agenda.

Enter FPP...

With none of the usual preliminaries or trappings, the Ministry staff simply gathered *en masse*, at one day's notice, and handed themselves over to a facilitator and the FPP ethos.

Having formed, this large and complex group certainly stormed.

But within two days, through incremental questions and expert helmsmanship in long and fiercely focussed sessions (hard core FPP!), they normed as five working groups, developed their problem statement, conducted a SWOT analysis, produced missions and logframes and—crucially—emerged as a high-performance team: proactive, informed, organised and confident.

Outcomes...

A subsequent review meeting between the Ministry and donors—which might otherwise have been a one-sided walkover or a confused confrontation—was an orderly, open-minded and balanced dialogue.

The Ministry team listened, responded, effectively presented, and emerged with clear ownership of their own way forward—the ingredient most likely to make things work. They had averted a crisis, mutually understood each other's issues, and enabled an agreed new basis for the ensuing planning process.

Clearly, FPP is highly flexible, adaptable and useful in a still-evolving range of contexts.

Section B

THE PRINCIPLES

4 The foundations

FPP evolves from four core concepts, and emerges with its own—to create effective teams which deliver their best possible work.

Concept 1: Awareness and empowerment

The all-stakeholders principle

Paulo Freire's "conscientization movement"—emphasising greater awareness and empowerment of oppressed and disadvantaged people—is credited with pioneering popular education methods (see Freire, 1970). In the 1960s, the Brazilian philosopher established an approach to enable the powerless to become organised, to articulate their needs and defend their rights. The emancipated learning that results is based on the principle of Action-Reflection-Action where each process is used to build up the concept of people's right to defend themselves against manipulation and oppression.

FPP translates this to the all-stakeholder principle, in which every voice counts, and the technique of incremental questions.

Concept 2: Learning by doing

Discovering answers

Experiential learning associated with Orlando Fals Borda of Colombia (Fals Borda and Rahman, 1991) emphasises multi-dimensional thinking (cognitive), feeling (affective) and acting (psycho-motor). This school of thought is credited with developing "learning by doing" methods associated with Participatory Action Research (PAR) of the 1980s which began with the research methods of Kurt Lewin, a German immigrant to the United States (Chambers, 1997).

This approach brings local people's knowledge and wisdom to the process, and underpins FPP's insistence that planning must involve the implementers from the outset, and the process of discovering (not imposing!) answers through incremental questions.

Concept 3: Visualisation

The mental/physical bridge

Visualisation is basically a mental bridge between a thought and a thing, and is older than—indeed the precursor of—language itself. Modern visualisation techniques in the FPP context originate from the Quickborn team of Germany associated with Eberhard Schnelle and his colleagues, who designed training in which decision makers and those affected by them visualise their problems, needs and solutions together, resulting in common action (Schnelle, 1997). The methods became popular in the 1970-1980s. This school contributes the use of mobile cards of different colours and shapes in visualising problems, needs and solutions, and the use of a moderator who provides methodological leadership.

This puts the F in FPP, and guides both the principle of teamwork and the visualisation techniques used in FPP.

Concept 4: Creative group processes

Building effective teams

Use of visualisation in participatory programmes was refined in the early 1990s by a team led by Neil McKee. McKee had learned a variety of participatory techniques from Hermann Tillman and Maruja Salas, which he introduced to the planning processes for social mobilisation and communication in UNICEF programmes in Bangladesh (McKee *et al.*, 2000). The techniques were adapted to local culture and found to be very effective in breaking down hierarchical relationships and stimulating creative group processes. The methods found their way into regular meetings, training and other events at various levels and were formalised as "Visualization in Participatory Programs" (VIPP). The system made inroads into East Africa through an initial training in 1992 under the leadership of the UNICEF Regional Director for East and Southern Africa at the time (UNICEF, 1998) .

FPP develops this strand to transform collections of diverse individuals into effective teams.

> UNICEF identified the need for water-sealed latrines as a crucial component in a sanitation project in Bangladesh and committed considerable resources over an extended period to this eminently sensible and positive plan. But year after year, the targets for latrine construction were not met, and those which were built were not widely used.
>
> UNICEF had conducted professional research, developed a technical remedy and convinced the Bangladesh government of the merits of the scheme. However, they had not involved the ultimate users of the latrines—the key stakeholders—in the concept or the construction. What seemed like a well-conceived and fully agreed "plan" did not work. It was unilateral and hierarchical.
>
> Later, VIPP was used to bring together the scientists, the national officials and the local communities to devise a fully participatory plan. Thereafter, the same resources did achieve the construction targets, and usage increased from 10 per cent to 40 per cent (see McKee *et al.*, 2000).

5 Picking the people

The people who make the plan must be independent in spirit and diverse in talent. Both the specific choices, and the means of their selection, must reassure the champions/funders and inspire confidence in the stakeholders.

The cardinals are diversity, balance, and truly arm's length democracy. A very specific and strict selection system is needed to ensure this.

Task Force selection

A political minefield

The all-stakeholder principle of FPP greatly reduces—but does not completely remove—suspicion that a plan might be manipulated by some vested interest. After all, who decides who the stakeholders are, and who decides the representative for each one? Do those selections not influence the final outcome?

One of the great truths of free society applies: "...justice should not only be done, but manifestly and undoubtedly be seen to be done." (Lord Chief Justice Hewart, 1923). To achieve this, the champions/funders must somehow divorce themselves from the selection process so they cannot be accused of appointing cronies to push through their own agenda.

The principals must progressively and "manifestly" build internal confidence and external credibility in three steps:

1. The appointment of a facilitator. This choice of an *independent* expert—as both mentor and referee—immediately shows willingness to at least loosen the grip of hierarchy and sends an important signal within the institution itself of a new approach.

2. The appointment of an *independent* "Board of Selectors" to whom the principals then hand over control. The Board members, usually three to six people, are of such character and renown that both the principals and the stakeholders can be sure that the project is in safe hands.

3. In turn the Board selects, and then hands control to, an *independent* Task Force of stakeholders who will make the plan. These men and women will have diverse perspectives and talents, but will meet a common high standard of pre-determined personal credentials.

The facilitator must explain these essential steps to the principals at the outset, and can help guide the Board and Task Force selection phases.

The Board members must be senior, highly accomplished men and women who are widely known and trusted. While they may be outspoken and controversial, they are listened to because they are seen to consistently put national interests above vested interests. In short, a team of "Elders" or whatever other term caries the right meaning for the culture concerned (chiefs, seniors, sages, doyens...).

Before the Board members nominate anyone for the Task Force, they must specify the credentials for candidature—the range of professions, age, gender, personal attributes such as integrity, ethics and analytical or technical acumen, and whatever else they deem important for the specific planning task at hand.

Then, in line with these generic criteria, each Board member is invited to submit personal recommendations which are then consolidated as a single master list. The master list (which does not show who recommended who) is then circulated to each Elder with an option to "veto" candidates who, in their opinion, do not have the agreed credentials. Again, the veto is anonymous.

The final list (of slightly more than the total number required) is then submitted to the principals for their approval and/or further veto but, for obvious reasons, not for addition of their own choices.

This is the usual and recommended selection process. Exceptionally, it may be necessary or more appropriate to let stakeholders themselves recommend Task Force members. In this version, the CEOs of stakeholder institutions constitute the Board. This option is less pure, more complex, and usually requires lengthy facilitated sessions. However, as long as the principals are sincere in their listing of stakeholders invited to comprise the Board, a balanced result is quite possible. In either case, the same principles of establishing generic credentials and democratising the vote apply.

No system is perfect, but the combination of this independent selection panel, its own democratic short-listing system, and the equal-voice transparency of the FPP process itself, are probably as close as it is possible to get.

The selection of the Board and their selection of Task Force members is also led by questions! These guide the qualities of person being sought and give objective measure to the criteria of choice.

Selection criteria

Some key principles

The principles of Task Force make-up (which the Board should regard as its rules of selection) are:

- Draw from different stakeholders (including government, NGOs, academics, researchers, managers, professionals, service providers).
- Appoint each one as an individual, not representing any institution, and emphasise that it is them, in person, who is chosen. Substitutes will not be permitted at any time.
- Aim for multi-disciplinary diversity.
- Ensure a balance of age, gender and any other key cultural distinctions.

Diversity enriches the Task Force's resource; balance safeguards against polarisation; both "democratise" the input and outcome.

MIXED TEAMS...

Balance through diversity, even within peer groups, to enrich and democratise both input and outcome

Variables

Tailoring the Task Force

The principles and (still-evolving) methods of FPP are consistent, but must be tailored to each institutional setting and to the particular problems being faced in each case. Knowing all the techniques is one thing; knowing which one to use at each moment is quite another; delivering that choice to the character and mood of a particular group is yet another.

The first variable is the make-up of the planning group or Task Force. Diversity is essential, but this may be represented by an all-professional team with different views and disciplines, or by a wider spectrum ranging from academics and government officials to semi-literate village leaders.

Whatever option is chosen, the integrity of the selection process, the conduct of the Task Force, the final plan and its implementation must be beyond doubt.

FPP by professional peers

The cutting-edge option

This book focuses on the effectiveness of FPP by peers, especially within the health and research sectors. All participants in all the cited cases presented held university degrees and professional positions in diverse disciplines (many were medical doctors or held PhDs).

This evolution to using highly educated and professionally homogeneous participants has allowed earlier VIPP techniques to be streamlined, by applying cutting-edge questions at the outset and getting directly to the critical issues which capture immediate attention...and motivation. For this reason, conventional training session "games" designed to integrate culturally distinct participants were not necessary, though this book does include some exercises which focus specifically on teamwork, problem-solving or conflict resolution.

Informing the Task Force

Six key inputs

Democratic selection will ensure that the Task Force has all shades of opinion, but any planning process also needs objective and comprehensive facts. FPP provides for six main sources of information:

1. The **Task Force** itself will have a wealth of knowledge about many aspects of the subject. Each member brings different knowledge and experience so participants can learn much from each other. Though this potential is often doubted at first, through the course of an FPP event it gains paramount recognition.

2. **Studies** can be commissioned to fill in specific data gaps. These may draw on existing databases or engage a consultant to conduct literature reviews, situation analyses, policy interviews, or qualitative and/or quantitative surveys.

3. **Field visits** are an opportunity to learn from real life situations and experience. These involve in-country locations which Task Force members have not seen before, and can lead to more profound understanding of the subject and their task.

4. **Expert witnesses** can be called to answer specific (usually technical) questions. Clearly this requires another selection process, based on the area in which specialist knowledge is necessary, defining the desired characteristics of an "expert", and assessing whether the necessary skills are available nationally or only internationally. The person or panel finally chosen attends an FPP session to answer the Task Force's questions face-to-face, and is given an opportunity to sum up and offer opinion on questions that have not been asked.

5. **Comparator visits** to centres of international excellence broaden the horizon. For logistical and cost reasons, the Task Force usually delegates between two and four members to visit one or more globally renowned institutions and report back. The choice of institutions visited is guided by their relevance to subject and the particular qualities the Task Force seeks to examine. The delegation is armed with a template which ensures the results can be analysed for lessons most relevant to the FPP event's own complex challenges.

6. **A Sounding Board** of decision makers convened to assess the draft plan can improve the final product. The Sounding Board is made up of key decision makers of major stakeholders most directly impacted by the plan. The entire Task Force presents itself

and the plan, and interaction with the Sounding Board is managed as an FPP session, guided by the facilitator. This process both reassures the stakeholders and leads to a sharper plan.

See also Chapter 11.

6 All about questions

FPP sessions are driven by questions, and roll out through a combination of discussions, exercises and visualisation.

The facilitator has a toolbox of techniques to steer focus and mood, tackle problems and guide the group to results.

Incremental questions

The only way

How else do you get stakeholder concerns, ideas and perspectives other than by asking for them?

Discussion based on statements (by lecture or debate) railroads the subject matter, gives the topic a unilateral spin, and invites one person to reach and hard-sell a multi-step conclusion (which may be threatening to other interests) before anyone else gets a chance to think or speak.

Persuasive statements may exert undue influence, even if their ideas are flawed; poorly expressed statements may confuse, even if their concepts are sound; either type might intimidate or inflame response. At best, such discussion will reveal participants' reaction to one individual's opinion. Not their own ideas. Not proactive. The session and the mood of the whole process will become a clamorous contest.

Incremental questions are the over-riding technique of FPP: to approach, to guide, to focus, to develop and to resolve through questions...one question at a time. In the end, the group will develop a SWOT analysis and a log-frame without the jargon or high-powered terminology. This assures greater understanding, easier implementation, clearer monitoring and finally, sustainability...all of which is spread across the group rather than concentrated with a consultant or individual trained in log-frame preparation.

THERE BE DRAGONS...

Separate parts of an issue are less threatening than the whole picture, so they can be objectively discussed and understood

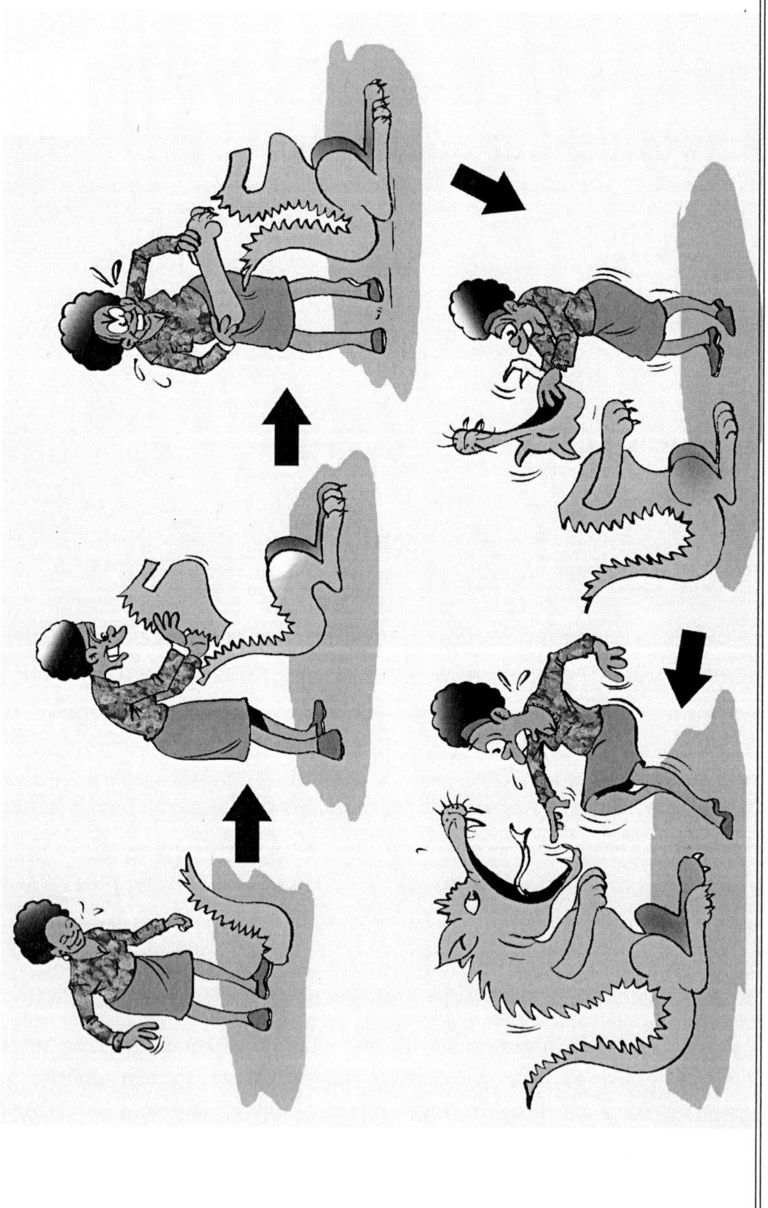

Questions—the right questions—invite a "blue-sky" response from any and every member of the group, neutrally and equally. They release and share information without teaching and preaching for the group to "see" a simultaneous cross-section of opinion.

Incremental questions—one step at a time—cannot confuse and do not threaten because they deal with just one isolated element, which on its own is inconclusive and therefore harmless, and thus more likely to get an objective answer.

Preconceptions and prejudices and vested interests attach to "final outcomes", not intermediate steps. Through incremental questions, by the time a series of objective answers and varied opinions and creative ideas are assembled into a significant "bigger picture", all have reached a broader and deeper understanding in a congenial atmosphere; prejudices and preconceptions have been reassessed and neutralised; vested interest has shifted from self to team.

FPP does not present argument, and then seek consensus by vote or by finding the lowest common denominator that participants *don't disagree* on. It platforms ideas and discussion, and seeks mutual agreement through understanding and teamwork. Questions—incremental questions—are the only way.

Building teamwork

Progressive transformation

VIPP techniques were developed to bring together diverse stakeholders from different levels of society in a common programme, with emphasis on participatory processes. FPP for complex organisations evolves these techniques to turn a more homogeneous (but highly competitive) set of stakeholders into an effective team.

Questions drive that process

The facilitator introduces the appropriate questions, employs participatory techniques and promotes group understanding. This builds incrementally towards effective, high-performance teams for both planning and implementation.

Stakeholders learn and remember through answering questions, "doing" and "saying" and jointly finding practical solutions to problems they have mutually prioritised.

Centrality of the question

Mastering destinies

The central thesis of Paulo Freire, a Brazilian educationalist who wrote *Pedagogy of the Oppressed and Cultural Action for Freedom* (Freire, 1970) is that unless the oppressed become subjects *and masters* of their own lives, no real development is possible.

The typical forum for his radical approach is a group of 20-25 people. Instead of a teacher, they have an organiser. Instead of lecturing, they have dialogue. Instead of being students, they are participants. Instead of an alienating syllabus, they have the real-life situations of the participants, divided into elements and presented in "codified" learning units.

Reading the picture

Giving life to thought

Freire's "conscientization" bases education on participants' own analysis of their own reality—*their* needs, potential, hopes and aspirations. As they become more aware, so they are encouraged to take action (Freire, 1970).

In practice, groups are presented with a picture that relates to their life situation. The picture has been constructed to pose a problem that immediately provokes reflection and discussion. Participants "read" the picture by gradually uncovering the social and economic conflicts it contains and by interpreting it on the basis of their own experience. Through this process, personal experience is articulated and verbalised. Through reflection and dialogue, latent knowledge—previously hidden as inklings and feelings—is brought to the surface. For the first time in the participants' lives, forces acting on them can be described; named.

When phenomena get named, they can be captured by thought. (How, for example, would you think about or act on "chivalry" if the word did not exist?) And when such named things are subjected to critical reflection (questioned!), they can be understood in their complex relations.

Why haven't you thought of this before?

How did this happen?

Who benefits?

Which interrelation exists between them?

What can we do?

When should we do it?

The very purpose (and process) of "conscientization" is to capture gut feelings in words, so they can be expressed, understood, thought through, and acted on. The process is driven by questions. At this very low level of verbalisation, the right questions are posed initially by a picture. In FPP's "visualisation", card clusters are, in a sense, this initial picture. The group paints it, by answering a question, and then interrogates it, by asking more questions (Newstrom and Scannell, 1998).

Types of questions

An open and shut case

There are many types of questions but, broadly, they can be classified as either closed or open-ended.

- Closed questions have definite answers or a limited range of possible responses. They solicit factual or specific information and are often, though not always, based on what, where, who and when. They rely on memory—the answer is recall of a known fact. In teaching method they are also called convergent questions. An example: *What is the title of this book?*

- Open-ended questions, on the other hand, can elicit many different responses, all of which may be valid. Such questions rely on thinking, reflection and critical analysis. They are often but not exclusively based on how and why. Because of the diversity of responses possible from them, they are also called divergent questions. For instance: *Why is facilitation useful in planning sessions?*

Beyond these basic categories, there are other types, such as:

- Leading questions which direct the respondent to expected answers. *You are going to attend the workshop, aren't you?*
- Rhetorical questions which have obvious answers that do not need to be stated (Am I right or am I right?). When an answer is desired, the question is often preceded with conditional statements which direct the responder: *All of us are convinced that FPP is more effective than traditional seminar processes, aren't we?*
- Probing questions which seek more information and clarification from statements already made. *What is the evidence that participatory facilitation is more effective? Where has it been used successfully?*
- Simple questions which are phrased to ask for one response at a time. For instance: *What is participatory facilitation?*
- Compound questions which ask for a variety of responses. For instance: *How has participatory facilitation been used in Africa, where, when and with what results?*

Qualities of a good question

The aim sets the design

It should immediately be clear that effective questions will tend to be simple rather than compound, open-ended rather than closed, and probing rather than leading or rhetorical.

With experience, facilitators develop an instinctive knack for asking effective questions, either orally or in writing. Such questions will be:

- Clear to the stakeholder, no need for repetition.
- Short.
- Specific on the information required.
- Relevant to the occasion and topic.
- Simply and appropriately worded.

OPEN QUESTIONS...
Get more open-minded answers

- Culturally sensitive, in terms of gender, ethnicity etc.
- Result-orientated—meant to lead to the eventual solutions.
- Reproductive—form a basis for generating more questions.

Conversely, questions will tend to fail when they are:

- Verbose—wordy, long winded.
- Bombastic—full of complex or high-sounding words.
- Vague—unclear in intention.
- Ambiguous—prone to different interpretations.
- Dead-ended—receive answers which do not justify further questions.
- Outside the scope of the respondents.
- Vindictive to the participants.
- Patronising—intended to demean participants and make them appear inadequate or incompetent.
- Opinionated—reveal the attitude (particularly if negative) of the facilitator.

In designing questions, it is always crucial to bear in mind the purpose. Among other things, we ask questions to:

- Get specific information.
- Improve understanding.
- Get clarification.
- Seek opinions, experiences and perspectives.
- Motivate thinking and generation of solutions.

7 Do's and don'ts

> There are no easy fixes or shortcuts—in time, cost, commitment or courage.
>
> The principles are crucial. The task is considerable. But the value of the result is incomparable.

Each FPP "event" may engage or bypass a great many "techniques" to suit its context, but both concept-logic and experience show that certain rules are immutable.

The group

The group must be:

Horizontal: Represent the perspectives and voices of all stakeholders.

Empowered: With absolute confidence in that authority.

Democratic: Free of hierarchy, either formal or implied. Every voice counts—equally.

The sessions

The sessions must be:

Informal: Relaxed, outside the box, free of teacher/learner demarcations.

Unpredictable: To avoid premeditation, heighten anticipation, stimulate by surprise.

Interactive: All participating, 'learning by doing'.

Flexible:	Responsive to mood and emerging case-by-case dynamics.
Multi-sensory:	Engage sight, sound, physical activity and involvement.
Congenial:	Non-competitive, respectful, free of jargon or cliquism.
Positive:	Team commitment to joint action, sure of success.
Relevant:	All action—however varied—always focused on the task.

The process

The process must be:

Question-based:	For many vital reasons (see Chapter 6).
Progressive:	Develop step by step, with incremental questions.
Continuous:	Dialogue-driven, through emergent new questions.
Patient:	Let the group adjust, discover and develop its potential (see Chapter 8).
Patient [sic]:	Let the questions guide the solutions, and set the pace.
Team-based:	Synergy, everyone helping everyone else.
Facilitated:	With expert skill and experience.

The Rationale

The key elements of FPP respond to how the human psyche works (UNICEF, 1998):

We learn	**We remember**
1% through taste	10% of what we read
2% through touch	20% of what we hear
3% through smell	30% of what we see
11% through hearing	50% of what we see and hear
83% through sight	80% of what we say
	90% of what we say and do

Contemplate this carefully: "What I hear I forget. What I see I remember. What I do I know."

Jargon busting

Jargon can be a useful shortcut in homogeneous groups, but by definition it expresses established concepts and therefore inhibits fresh thinking (which is what brainstorming is supposed to produce). It is by nature cliquish, so in diverse groups it tends to exclude rather than include; at best it can be misunderstood, and at worst it can intimidate. FPP can have none of it.

JARGON BUSTING...

Highbrow techno brilliance is not impressive...it is confusing

For example, certainly FPP will include "logframe" and "SWOT" and "results-orientated planning" elements, but it will not use these terms nor explain what they mean. Because the same result can be achieved, more simply, more clearly and more certainly, through incremental questions:

What are the strengths of...?

What are the weaknesses of...?

What are the opportunities of...?

What are the threats of...?

What is the objective of...?

Who is to do what...?

What inputs do we need...?

What is the expected outcome...?

How will the output be measured and monitored...?

What are the assumptions...?

Knowledge sharing *versus* teaching

Learning defines a process of acquiring knowledge and skills. It presumes the presence of a central source of that knowledge (teacher) and recipients of that knowledge (learners). The success of the teaching is often proved by giving the learner a test. The judgment of the "right" answer is predetermined and unilateral.

In FPP, there is no teach-learn distinction. FPP is more a problem-based process. Each participant contributes and acquires knowledge; together they decide the aims, mutually discover/assemble the necessary information and ideas; and the right answer is not known in advance, by anybody. It has to be found, by all. It is what all agree on.

The facilitator manages the human interaction that achieves that informed common result. The facilitator will think through and choose the methods that will lead to productive discussions in a mutual and non-competitive atmosphere. The aim is not to prove how much learning has taken place (by exams), but to generate workable solutions to recognised problems (a plan). Emphasis is placed not on individual excellence but on group cohesion, collective attitudes and agreement. The ultimate goal is to create a culture of teamwork that guarantees sustainable processes, relevant results and horizontal organisation for more effectiveness and efficiency.

Leadership *versus* pecking order

Leadership is often mistakenly equated with hierarchy. If there is a leader, then there must be followers.

FPP debunks this misperception. People who set the agenda (even with wisdom) and drive the process (even with charisma) and impose the result which they want or believe to be best (even with group welfare at heart) are not leaders. They are dictators.

Leadership, in its proper sense—and all enlightened CEOs and deans and chairpersons will subscribe to this definition—means to "inspire and enable others to perform to their highest individual potential in the common interest"...of a team, a group, a department, a company, an institution.

GOOD LEADERSHIP...
Is not about being in charge; it's about optimising teamwork

It is therefore possible—and preferable—for every member of a group to demonstrate the qualities of leadership, simultaneously, and without subordinating anybody else to the status of follower. In successful FPP, each member of the planning group inspires and enables every other. The multiplier effect on group performance is logarithmic!

Advantages

These principles have evolved because they are either essential, or optimally useful in: tapping people's knowledge and experience; ensuring equal opportunity; generating spontaneous, creative and innovative ideas; handling complicated topics incrementally through basic components; getting diverse individuals to work as a team, to learn from and respect one another, and commit to joint action.

FPP generates home-grown solutions (there are no "consultants"); provides quick reports, and delivers a plan developed by a team through agreement and owned by the stakeholders, which, axiomatically, can be more readily implemented.

Challenges

The FPP process is time consuming, and time is not cheap. There are no shortcuts (see Chapter 8).

Though the plan is made by and belongs to the stakeholders themselves, the facilitator plays a crucial role in enabling them to deliver their best performance and the optimum result—through experienced, perceptive, communicative, highly organised, efficient and diplomatic guidance of group dynamics, retreat/session structure, and use of visualisation and other techniques.

For participatory planning to be effective, it is imperative that the facilitators are well trained at the outset, have opportunities to practice and gain experience through co-facilitation with a master trainer, and prepare carefully whenever on assignment.

FPP is likely to be alien to and resisted by those more familiar with fixed pre-workshop programmes, paper presentations, board room set-ups, session chairs, hierarchical procedures and protocol, as well as "fix-it" consultants with their huge, glossy reports.

Participatory processes must bear in mind that FPP by professional peer groups involves well-educated professionals who are "loaded" with preconceptions, prejudices, strong opinions...and the hierarchy habit, in which they expect to enjoy influence by authority and to get their own way.

Section C

TECHNIQUES

8 Tuning the talk

There are numerous techniques by which the facilitator can change the focus and mood, to ensure nobody hides, nobody is ignored, nobody dominates, to calm things down or liven things up.

All of these also constantly "inform" the group.

Discussion, in one form or another, is almost constant in FPP sessions, but there are many variations of how it is conducted. Also—and very importantly—the character of a group changes (always!) as an FPP event progresses, and facilitation needs to adjust accordingly. This chapter provides a menu of techniques, each designed to help optimise performance...whatever the stage or situation.

The pattern of change from the first day to the last is so common and predictable that it has a name:

"Forming, storming, norming, performing" (Tuckman, 1965)

Forming

When a group first gets together, all members are busy sizing up the situation and each other—a natural social reflex when faced with the unknown. The hallmarks are "caution" and "courtesy", which is good for ensuring peace but rotten for generating ideas and frank discussion. Facilitators recognise that this phase is necessary and unavoidable, but use get-to-know-you techniques ("ice-breakers") to accelerate the process.

Storming

Those early inhibitions break down faster than team spirit builds up, so in the second phase the group becomes a collection of more confident but

FORMING...

With courtesy and caution

STORMING...

A fight about might and right

still polarised individuals. Again this is a natural and necessary process—not a cause for concern, but potentially a cause for control. A self-imposed code of conduct helps prevent the tensions getting out of hand, and techniques to promote calm and co-operation come to the fore.

Norming

Once familiarity overcomes inhibition and the angst has been aired (and not before), the group is ready to knit as a team. Everyone is still an individual, but with mutual recognition and respect for each other's value and their common goal. The facilitator uses techniques to consolidate the harmony; to reinforce the concept that unity is not only possible but in fact much more powerful and productive. A high-performance team is in the making.

NORMING...
Recognising the validity and value of other points of view

Performing

In the later stages of an FPP event, the team gets into top gear—ready to harness and prove all its synergy and skill as a unit—and produces the result. Problems that may have been shelved as intractable at the start can now be solved—often remarkably easily.

PERFORMING...
Working as an effective team

The key message here is that these phases are normal; necessary. The facilitator needs to smooth their progress, but they are not cause for concern. Indeed, they are positive indicators that the process is on track!

Throughout, the facilitator has an arsenal of techniques to steer the process phase by phase and hour by hour, tailored to the needs of any given moment.

These include particular information-gathering exercises itemised in Chapter 5 (field visits, expert witness, studies, comparator visits etc.). But remember, the Task Force itself is the primary and most prolific source of information and ideas. It is the facilitator's job to ensure this potential is maximised by using techniques that optimise cohesion, relevance, creativity, energy, mood.

9 Games and exercises

Generic elements

The use of games and exercises is not as important to homogeneous groups of academics and researchers as it is to diverse groups often involved in VIPP processes. However, to enhance the collegial ambience or to provide learning scenarios, useful games and exercises can be categorised as:

- Ice-breakers: To help strangers feel comfortable with each other, and to dismantle hierarchies.
- Warm-ups: In the morning, to get participants mentally and physically charged-up.
- Energisers: As interludes, to sustain energy levels and break monotony.
- Messengers: To illustrate aspects of communication...and miscommunication.
- Inventors: To bring out the creative potential of one and all.
- Team builders: To create a sense of togetherness and eliminate unhealthy competition and conflict.
- Sensitisers: To make participants aware of gender, cultural, religious and ethnic issues and how they affect our lives.
- Games for fun: Pure and simple.
- Solvers: To demonstrate approaches to tackling problems and the difference between solo and group attempts.
- Relaxers: For meditation.

- Eye-openers: To explore "perceptions", and how and why people look at and interpret the same thing differently.
- Ceasefires: To reduce tensions and resolve disagreements.
- Evaluators: To provide feedback on the value of the sessions.

The distinction between a game and an exercise is not crucial—indeed, they overlap and blur. Broadly, games prioritise fun and can be harmlessly competitive while they deliver their message or serve their purpose. Exercises are also intended to be enjoyable, but their priority is to deliver a specific insight or understanding.

A good exercise may bear one, some or all of the following qualities:

- Involves everyone in the group.
- Helps advance the group process.
- Creates group synergy.
- Creates best atmosphere for participation and learning.
- Provides a common ground for group experience.

A good game or exercise may contain one, some or all of the following qualities:

- Enhances the democratic spirit of participatory processes.
- Reduces dominance by loud and outspoken participants.
- Is adaptable to different socio-cultural contexts.
- Is usable with a wide variety of groups.
- Is gender (etc.) sensitive.
- Is culturally appropriate.
- Is not too long.

However, games and exercises should:

- Not take precedence over the core business of the workshop.

- Be slotted in judiciously bearing in mind the time of the day and the intended effect.
- Be purposeful and have clearly stated instructions.

Most-effective exercises

The following exercises were selectively and carefully used among senior academics and established researchers:

Introduction and ice breaking

Mutual interview: Pair-off the participants (avoiding combinations who are already good friends). Ask them to talk to one another about themselves and to record the information on a card. They will use this card to introduce the partner to the group. The topic of discussion could vary—my past, present and future in planning; my unique characteristics etc. The exercise helps reveal things hitherto unknown to the others and also helps participants explore and verbalise their identities and to talk about others in the planning group (UNICEF, 1998).

True...false: Ask each participant to write on a card three things about themselves. Two of the things should be true but one should be false. Each participant reads out the cards and the plenary tries to identify the false one. The exercise is useful if participants already know one another very well and helps them to find out even more about personal details—number of family members, hobbies, marital status, illness, special honors, etc. (Dodge *et al.*, 2002).

Communication

Buzz groups: All participants are divided into groups of two or three, and each group discusses a given topic and captures its points on cards. This is a very useful method of generating quick ideas and prioritising them. The process is called "buzz" groups because once everyone in the room is talking, the sound effect is similar to that of bees.

The whisper: The facilitator whispers a statement to one participant (so quietly that no one else can hear it) and asks the participant to whisper what s/he heard to the next participant who does the same to the next,

BUZZ GROUPS...
Lead to a hive of activity

and so on until all participants are covered. The last participant then says aloud what s/he heard. This is compared with the original statement by the facilitator. Debriefing discusses why the final statement turns out to be different from the original. The exercise helps illustrate the problems of oral communication and hence the need for visualisation and recording and deliberations.

Concentration

A farmer's hen: Seat participants in the standard plenary formation. Let the first say: "A farmer's hen has laid an egg." The second participant asks the first "A what?" and the first answers "An egg." The second participant then tells the third participant about the farmer's hen. When the third asks the second "A what?," the second relays the same to the first and the answer is relayed forwards again. This goes on until all participants are covered. Ask participants that when they come to say "an egg", they should do it in their mother tongue. The exercise helps to hype concentration and co-ordination, and also celebrates the linguistic diversity in the group.

Walkabout: This is an exploratory method, which allows participants to discuss a topic outdoors as they walk. They are not allowed to stand or sit, and do not record anything. It helps unleash creativity and generates diverse views. It is best used to "wake up" a session; often in that soporific after-lunch period!

Group dynamics

Cow trader: Write the following statements and read them out to participants. "A cow trader buys a cow for $60 and then sells it for $70. He regrets and buys the cow back for $80. But since he is a trader, he sells it again for $90."

In plenary, ask each participants to mentally calculate the profit of the trader, write the answer on a card and put it in their pocket.

Then divide participants into groups (of about 5 people each) and ask them to discuss the answers.

They should return to plenary when everyone in the group is convinced about one correct answer for their group.

The mathematical answer does not matter. Debrief by asking participants to describe what behaviours were exhibited by individuals as they tried to solve the problem. The results should be used to draw relevant lessons on how people behave in groups and how to overcome the problems associated with such dynamics.

The facilitator should not focus on the answer, only on the process. (McKee, 1993).

Problem solving

Debates: Opted for and conducted with care to comply with FPP's "non-competitive" principles—allow participants to articulate opposing viewpoints on controversial issues. A debate can be structured in different formats such as conventional pro-contra, trial scenes, value clarification etc.

Nine dot problem: Issue the nine dot handout (see diagram) to each participant and ask them to individually join all the dots with only four, straight, connected lines and without lifting the pen from the paper from the start of the pattern to the end. Walk around and check who has done it right. Then ask those who have the correct solution to explain to the others. If none has it right, explain the solution and display the complete figure yourself. Ask participants what made the exercise difficult, what assumptions they made and why they never thought of drawing outside the imaginary boundaries. Debrief on the lesson: that we often fail to get solutions to problems because we restrict our thinking to the known rather than exploring extended frontiers ("thinking outside the box") (UNICEF, 1996).

NINE-DOT DIAGRAM

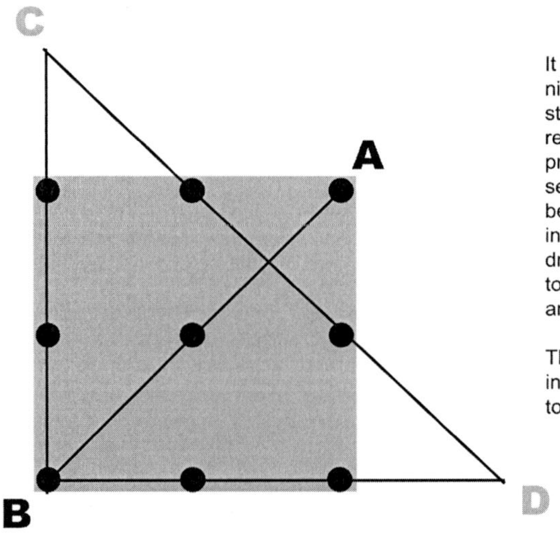

It is not possible to join all nine dots with four continuous straight lines if the lines are restrained within the grey area proscribed by the dots themselves (the box). The task can be achieved only by extending the lines "outside the box", drawing first from A to B, then to external points C and D (or D and C) and back to B.

The graphic illustration of thinking outside normal assumptions to solve a problem is profound.

Role plays: A role play is a short, illustrative, dramatic scene used to explore a specific question. Participants "act" specific personalities in classical roles. Role plays often enable comedy and laughter around sensitive and serious issues. For example, academics might be asked to tackle the issue of administrative bureaucracy from the students' perspective. (The I@mak.com cast a sterotypical, old-fashioned professor as a modern cybertech student!)

The six-step problem solving: Ask participants to brainstorm on several conflict situations they have experienced—between staff members, between a senior and a junior, between neighbours etc. Divide them into groups and ask each group to role-play the situation with plenary as audience. Ask the audience to help them solve the problem and note down the steps to the solution. Then display the six-step problem-solving handout (prepared by the facilitator in advance) and ask each group to replay their scenario, following the steps. In plenary, evaluate the efficacy of the six-step process.

Step 1—Identify needs: What is it that you need or want? Each person in the conflict should answer this question without blaming or accusing the other person.

Step 2—Define the problem: What do you think the problem here is? Other individuals can help answer, but the people in the conflict must agree to the definition of the problem.

Step 3—Brainstorm solutions: Can you think of a way that we might solve this problem? Anyone may offer response. Suggestions should be written down without comment or judgment. The aim of this step is to come up with as many solutions as possible.

Step 4—Evaluate the solutions: Would you be happy with this solution? Each party in the conflict goes through the list of alternatives and says which ones would or would not be acceptable to them.

Step 5—Decide on best solution: Do you both agree to this solution? Is the problem solved? Make sure both parties agree and acknowledge their efforts in working out the conflict.

Step 6—Check how the solution is working: Can we talk again soon to make sure that the problem is really solved? A plan should be made of how to evaluate the solution. The evaluation may take place later that day, the next day, week etc., depending on the nature of the conflict (UNICEF, 1996).

Hot seats: This is another method for generating ideas. Participants sit in a large circle of chairs facing inwards to a couple of empty "hot seats". Anyone who wishes to speak must go to a hot seat to make a statement or enter discussion with someone sitting on the other hot seat(s). It is particularly useful for discussing controversial issues and giving people an open forum for airing views.

Perception

Squares: Issue the squares handout (see diagram) to each participant and ask them to say how many squares they see. Ask them to explain how they came to that answer. After some time, it will be discovered that there are 30 squares in the grid and not 16 or so that they see more immediately. Debrief on why people perceive the same things differently and how to deal with that in a group process (UNICEF, 1998).

The answer to the "how many different squares" question is 30.

16 of 1 small square each, as per grid
9 of 4 small squares each (2x2)
4 of 9 small squares each (3x3)
1 of 16 small squares each (4x4)

Decision-making strategies

Decision-making cards: The facilitator prepares in advance, but keeps concealed, seven cards, each depicting one of the following decision-making strategies:

- **The leader decides:** The group chooses a leader. The leader hears what everyone thinks. Then the leader decides what the group will do.

- **Chance decision:** The group flips a coin to choose what it will do.
- **Consensus decision:** Each member of the group selects one choice or solution. The group members listen to each other's rationale. Then they come to an agreement on which one they will use.
- **Compromise decision:** Everybody in the group agrees to give up a little of what they want to come to a solution that is acceptable to everyone.
- **Voting decision:** Several choices are suggested. Group members say which one they like. The choice most people like is the one the group chooses.
- **Expert decision:** The person in the group who knows most about the subject or problem makes the decision for the group.
- **Arbitration decision:** The group asks an outsider to make a decision for them. The group agrees to do whatever the outsider decides.

Divide participants into seven small groups and ask them to brainstorm on different ways of decision-making that they know. List the methods they suggest on a chart.

Then issue each group with one of the facilitator's pre-prepared cards and ask them to use that strategy to make a decision on the following:

"Imagine that your organisation has received a grant from a donor of some US$ 100,000 and you are charged with deciding on how to use this money. Use the strategy allocated to come to a decision."

After about 15 minutes, ask each group to indicate the decision made and briefly evaluate the differences. Then debrief on whether the members felt their assigned strategy was efficient in achieving a good decision, its advantages and disadvantages and whether everyone felt satisfied. Then describe all of the strategies and ask plenary to rank them.

Emphasise that any of the strategies (or a combination of two or more) might be applicable in different situations, depending on the nature of the decision to be made (UNICEF, 1996).

Assessment exercises

Voting by the feet: Draw a grid on the floor marking percentage ranges (0-25%, 26-50%, 51-75%, 76-100%). Participants will be asked to stand against the rating that captures their evaluation of different aspects of a process which will be mentioned by the facilitator, one by one. After each aspect is mentioned, participants move to their chosen ranking line. The number standing against each scale is counted and recorded. When all the aspects have been covered, ranked by this line-up voting, and recorded, transfer the results onto a grid on the board and summarise the general trend from the exercise.

Cobweb commitments: At the end of a planning event, ask participants to stand in a circle. One participant holds a ball of string. That participant states a personal commitment to implement the decisions arrived at, and then—firmly holding the end of the ball of string—lobs the (unraveling) ball to any other participant in the circle. The catcher makes an equivalent statement of commitment, firmly holds the free line of string, lobs the ball to another participant, and so on until all participants have spoken and ... the lines of string from, to and between each participant form a cobweb of lines. This is used to emphasise the unity of the group in fulfilling their commitments and realising the plan. It also illustrates the complexity of relationships required for success (McKee, 1993).

One dot question: Draw a triangle and mark the corners with "Yes" (Fully Agree); "No" (Disagree); and "Partly" (Agree). Supply each participant with a circular adhesive label (dot). The facilitator then makes an evaluation statement, and asks participants to place their dot next to the angle which concurs with their view of the statement (McKee, 1993).

Teamwork

Ask participants to suggest one long word which describes the planning process they are involved in. Once they have agreed on the word, impose a "no talking" condition and ask them each to:

- Personally predict how many other words of three letters or more they can derive using only (but not necessarily all) the letters contained in the long word, and to write their prediction at top right of their own sheet of paper.

BALLOT BLOCKS...
The one dot vote can help reveal preferences and priorities

- Then allow three minutes for them to derive as many words as they can, working alone. Let them personally compare their actual and predicted scores, but not declare them.
- Then ask everyone to estimate how many different words they think the whole group has derived, and post these predictions on cards.
- Next get one person to report the words s/he found, and write them on a flip chart. Ask the next person to add any words s/he found that are not already on the flip chart, and go around the room until everyone has added their extra words to the list.
- Then compare the number of words they achieved individually and the number they estimated the group tally would be, with the actual group result.

This exercise demonstrates that, working alone, the best single performer tends to get about 50 per cent of the group total. Discuss the reasons for this and explain how working together generates more and better results.

Such a word game obviously works best in the peer group context where participants have roughly equal literacy levels, but even if one member of the group turns out to be a world Scrabble champion, much amusement is added but the message is not lost.

Take-offs and landings

In one way, conducting an FPP session is like flying an aircraft—the most critical moments are take-off and landing. The journey cannot progress until the group is "off the ground", elevation must be sustained by energisers through the day, and at the close of session the group should not be left "up in the air".

Sessions should never just fizzle out. They should close on an upbeat (ready for tomorrow's take-off) with a purposeful thought to take forward. Exercises and games can deliver both the conclusive moment and the point to ponder. Facilitators can use this to repair or prepare the mood for the following day.

WORLDLY WISE...

The inside-out exercise transforms participants into advocates

An excellent example for the very end of a programme is the "inside-out" message: "that participants must take what they have learned in the programme out into the wider world."

Steps:

- Ask all participants to stand in one large circle, facing inwards.
- Ask them to place their right arms across their stomachs, so the middle of their forearm is resting against their navel.
- Then likewise the left arm, so their arms form an X over their midriff.
- Then ask them to link hands, using their left hand to link with the person on their right, and their right hand to link with the person on their left.
- While thus joined, ask each in turn to make a positive statement about what they have gained from the programme.
- When all have spoken (inwards, towards each other), stress the need to take those messages outside, and...
- ...while still holding hands, ask them all to turn and face outwards (which they can do without breaking the links, by raising their left arm and ducking underneath their own elbow).

The fact that turning inside out is possible without breaking the chain is surprising...and memorable. The physical symbolism—simply but powerfully—gives the message special impact.

Nutcrackers

Here is a taste of some of the exercises commonly used during core discussion when ideas, agreement or energy stalls.

Brainstorming: This refers to quick generation of ideas without censorship. The facilitator poses a question and ideas are shouted out at random. Any of the participants can respond and the ideas are captured by co-facilitators on cards. This generates ideas in a similar manner to

NUTCRACKERS...

Ways to resolve intractable problems

card writing and is employed when time is running out and ideas need to be collected fast to assure continuation of a train of thought.

Fish bowl: Participants form two equal groups—one forming an inner circle (facing outwards) and the other an outer circle around it (facing inwards)—and each participant has a face-to-face discussion with the person opposite. Every few minutes the circles rotate, generating fresh face-to-face partnerships in "speed dating" fashion. This can be used to break deadlock in a plenary session or to enliven the proceedings with physical activity. It accelerates the individual get-to-know-you process.

Scenario: A scenario is a real-life situation (factual or simulated) which illustrates what happened in a particular circumstance, that can be "studied" to analyse problems and their consequences, examine relationships among variables, open room for debate, and lead to logical conclusions.

The method is useful to work out, in detail, a way to define and analyse a problem, develop real solutions, make proposals, and list activities from which general conclusions can be drawn.

A scenario can be presented in different forms: oral (narration, drama), written, visual (picture, slides) and audio-visual (video, PowerPoint or film). The main advantages of case studies are that they are easy to relate to, illustrative, grounded in reality, trigger critical thinking, are inherently problem-solving, and allow diverse perception to be expressed.

Scenario exercises must be prepared in detail by the facilitator in advance.

10 Seeing what you have said

Once a group is thinking and talking, the ideas must be captured, ordered, presented, analysed...quickly, simply and without disrupting the flow. FPP has a central mechanism that does all that—and more.

Visualisation

The most common and popular "visualisation" is handwritten cards displayed on one or more large pinboards. This is a core technique to quickly gather ideas from participants on a particular topic or to capture the keynotes of any discussion. It creates a simple visual presentation which everyone can intuitively understand at first glance.

Large pinboards—about 6 ft × 3 ft (180 cm × 90 cm) as a balance between space and portability—are placed at an unobstructed focal point. They are made of softboard for easy insertion and extraction of map pins, and mounted on stands so their tops can be reached by people of average height, and their bases can be seen by those seated at the back of the room.

Every pinboard has a "title"—a question or topic written by the facilitator at the start of a session on a long card and pinned centre top.

While participants are thinking about the question, the facilitator pins a row of distinctively coloured blank cards for column or "cluster" headings.

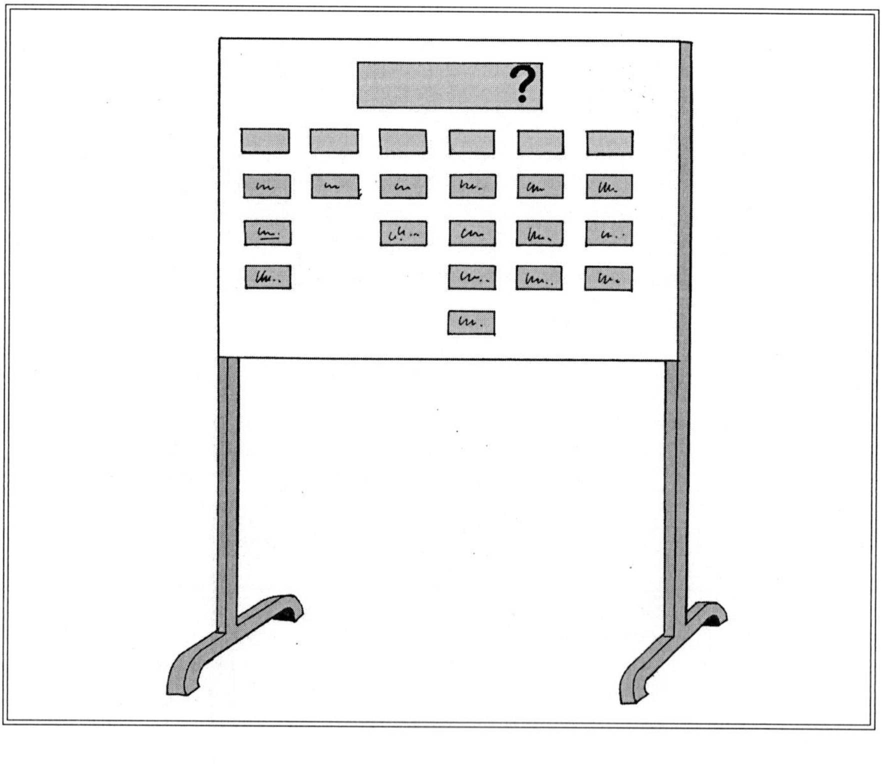

Participants write their ideas on "answer" cards, which are collected, shuffled, and then read out and pinned up one at a time. Participants decide which column each should go into, so those with similar content/ theme are clustered together.

When all the cards are in place, and their cluster positions have been verified, participants decide and write in the cluster headings. Clusters turn random ideas into identifiable issues/themes.

This technique can be employed at the start of a topic, and stimulate discussion based on what the cards and clusters indicate, or be used during or after discussion to capture outcomes...and to determine priorities and the next question.

Though the system is basic, it is vital to the FPP process and there are very specific design and use requirements—the size and colour of the cards, the thickness and colour of marker pens, rules for card content and hand-writing styles, and particular sequences of distribution, collection and display; all to ensure they do their job to the best effect.

Because this technique is used so frequently and constantly in FPP sessions, uniformity of use saves reinventing the wheel every time and allows the process to become second nature to all participants—hence the physical handling does not consume mind space.

The card system

To avoid confusion and assure legibility, it is important that everyone follows the card-writing rules:

- uses the same colour ink,
- writes boldly and neatly,
- writes only keywords and only one idea on each card,
- writes no more than three lines on each card,
- uses a normal mix of capital and small letters, preferably not joined up.

The need to readily fit many cards on the board (for example, number of participants × 2), and yet the need for writing on the cards to be legible from the far side of a room, determines a typical "answer card" size of about 10 cm × 20 cm—a large postcard.

Answer cards should be light coloured to ensure good contrast with pen colour, and be uniform. Colour should not make one answer more conspicuous (important?) than any other. Different colours or shapes should be used only when authors or answers are being purposefully categorised.

Title cards should be larger and consistently coloured so they have a distinctive identity and immediate recognition. A size of 10 cm × 50 cm is practical.

Cluster cards should be the same size as answer cards (10 cm × 20 cm) but have a contrasting and high-impact colour—after all, the cluster headings most succinctly rationalise individual thinking into group priorities for the next step, and are therefore the key (standout) element in the picture—the visualisation.

Steps

- The facilitator visualises (boldly writes) the question or topic on a long rectangular card (10 cm × 50 cm), pins it top and centre of a pinboard, confirms that everyone understands the meaning of the question, and clarifies any ambiguities.
- An equal supply of answer cards is distributed to each participant or buzz group—either uniform or colour-coded if categories are significant.
- While the participants are writing their cards—usually two, and up to four cards each—the facilitator can pin up the blank cards for later cluster headings.
- Participants think, and then write their cards silently, following the rules of writing. Allow adequate time for this.
- Completed cards are placed face down, for collection by helpers drawn from among the participants.
- The collectors shuffle all the cards, and then read them out—loudly, like an announcement—one at a time.

- Cards which are unclear in meaning or are improperly written should be rewritten immediately. In most cases, the problem will be illegibility, or cards that break the rules such as "only one" distinct idea per card.
- In turn, the helpers pin up each card in a straight column under one of the (blank) cluster heading cards—the plenary guides where each card should be clustered. Cards should not physically overlap.
- Cards which duplicate keywords or ideas should not be discarded but also be pinned up in line with the philosophy that every idea counts. In some cases, the repetition illustrates the importance participants attach to that particular idea.
- Once all the cards are pinned, appropriate cluster headings are verbally verified by plenary and written in by the helpers.
- The facilitator will then guide the plenary in reviewing the clusters.
- If the ideas are to be used further, clusters can be prioritised by getting participants to vote (using sticky labels) on which they think are most important. However, in most cases these boards are just saved or recorded, and are used as the material from which a smaller group refines and develops more fully considered themes, such as a problem statement.

Notes

Aesthetics are enhanced by leaving some empty space between cards and clusters. A chart that is overcrowded with cards is not appealing and is difficult to read, although it must always be recognised that the cluster title is the most important.

When doing card writing and collection, always bear in mind the number of participants. In the question, the facilitator can stipulate the number of cards per person, varying between one and four, to avoid too many cards which will take ages to cluster and use up all board space. If there are many participants e.g. over 20, it is advisable to do card writing in buzz groups to reduce the number of cards per participant and to partly prioritise responses from the outset.

Emerging technology

While the core principles of FPP endure, the technology around them is ever changing. The process has its own challenges and opportunities to keep up with.

The demands and opportunities of new technology are often a major reason why organisations seek to transform themselves in the first place—especially educational and research institutions. New technology can be part of the solution, too.

So it would be ironic indeed if FPP itself—the transforming process—was not techno-savvy in its own field.

The core principles of FPP are unlikely to change much or soon; they are, after all, based on human nature, which is enduring. The techniques FPP uses will be progressively refined but they, too, are founded on how the human psyche works. Always has. Still does. Possibly always will. Another constant.

What might change, quite dramatically, is how those techniques are delivered. An important and immediate example is the "cards and pin-boards" used for visualisation.

It works. It works well. It will continue to do so. It has the added merit of using materials and technology that are universally available. The manual process, though rudimentary and cumbersome, has its merits in the "doing" context.

But where higher-tech options are available and affordable, facilitators need to be up-to-speed and ready to explore new dimensions.

Zing

Today, the boards and cards and pens and pins can be replaced by a large screen and keyboards—which can do almost exactly the same job much more swiftly and flexibly. Zing is the pioneer of these computerised systems (*www.anyzing.com*).

Participants each have their own keyboard (or small groups can be in close reach) and the "cards" they type-in are displayed instantly (and anonymously) on the screen. Further, the software which enables that to happen can also record, rearrange and analyse the data any-which-way...at the press of a button.

Consider the impact of that on the visualisation experience, and on the ease of things like data capture and report production!

None of the case studies in this manual had access to Zing, and the intention is not to deliver an IT filibuster. Further, having explained all the principles, purposes and processes of visualisation using cards and pinboards, the essential ground has already been covered—even if this technique is now made electronic.

Facilitators can apply those principles, with minor logistical adjustments, to the screen and keyboard option with ease and confidence.

Both pinboards and screens are democratic (all participants are involved and heard and there is not a larger digital typeface for the boss), they stimulate ideas, table brutal facts, reveal patterns, decide priorities, free up minds, drill down on questions, and all-in-all help the facilitator to ensure group performance is at its best.

With the computer version, the facilitator's first role is to give participants the confidence and skills to use the keyboard, to express in bullet points and not to worry about grammar and spelling.

What might some of the new dimensions be? Well, endless. But as starter examples:

- Facilitators using Zing find that participants are braver about what they are ready to type than what they are prepared to write.
- Zing software includes a "a bank of golden questions" (while equally allowing the client and facilitator to generate their own).
- Other than as a substitute for "cards", the Zing system brings a computer, keyboards and screen into the environment. That could be used to invent and animate games and exercises, change the ambiance of a room, and bring opportunities for an always important part of any group activity—humour.

What else might that processing and display capacity be used to do…by a facilitator whose job, in large part, is to manage minds?

MindManager

MindManager (*www.mindjet.com/products/mindmanager*) is the name of another piece of software that can be used to map and track thought processes, automatically organise ideas, questions, elements etc., into a physical diagram. Quintessential "visualisation".

One example might be for working groups to tackle their assignments on this format, which could then be directly projected on big screen for presentation of their analysis to plenary. And on from there.

MindManager follows the principles of brainstorming, where the facilitator captures thoughts and cluster responses to agreed headings which are prioritised by the group. This technology manages that automatically, and can transform the presentation between tree, map and text formats in two clicks.

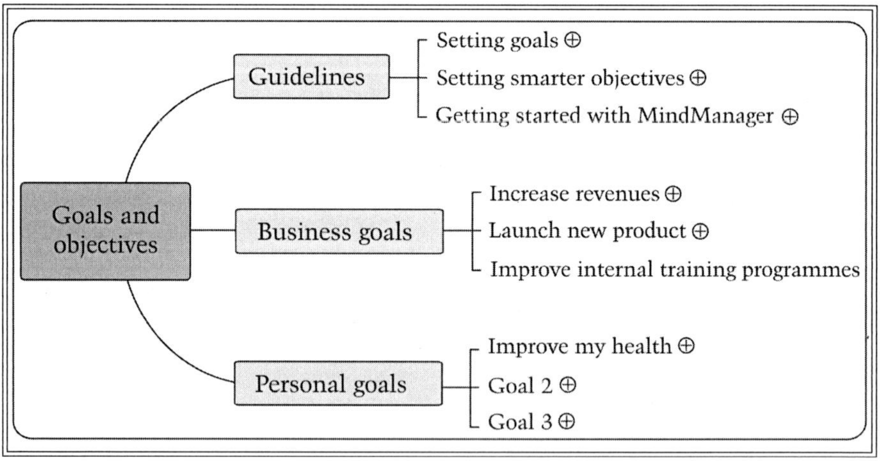

11 Walking the talk

> The task force itself contains a wealth of knowledge to discover and share. FPP then offers five more systems for gathering more information, and techniques for making the most of that know-how.

While the task force itself is the primary source of information, and the card system is the essential, central and predominant means of discovering and marshalling that know-how, more is needed: to stimulate creative thinking, to untangle the knottiest problems, to process the outcome of discussions, to build the team dynamic, and to gather and digest additional information.

In all (as noted in Chapter 5), there are six ways the group is informed:

1. Group dynamics.
2. Expert witness.
3. Commissioned studies.
4. Comparator visits.
5. Field visits.
6. Sounding board.

Group dynamics

Plenary

This is the foundation of all FPP processes, generating the "big picture" through questions, card writing and clustering. Differences...contrasting perspectives and divergence...are accepted but not allowed to degenerate into conflict, arguments and the "taking of sides".

Working groups

Small groups are formed and given separate tasks and locations (even going outside) to discuss, deliberate and prepare presentations based on the outcome of a plenary session.

Group work offers a stimulating change, intensifies interaction between participants, allows delegated exploration of many issues simultaneously, builds pockets of agreement, but most importantly allows greater depth and understanding of complex issues which cannot be dealt with through simple cards containing one idea and clustered into headings.

Questions addressed by working groups may include divergent perspectives and options. Working groups democratise processes and reduce competition. It is within working groups that most of the detailed and difficult work of writing out full and complete conceptual perspectives is done.

Presentations

Working groups use the same "visualisation" techniques to present their outcomes... from the problem statement, to the budget, to the logframe. Each working group will select its own chairperson, secretary and presenter, based not on hierarchy but on "talent" and "skills". Thus, it is the best communicator who makes the presentation, but varied creative techniques can be used.

Expert witnesses

Filling the gaps

During plenary discussion, participants encounter or realise gaps in their own knowledge, and need to interrogate an expert—on facts or concepts—to get the information they need to compose a plan.

A deeper look

The expert witness option has an advantage over commissioned studies or comparator visits in that it is interactive, not only answering pre-determined questions but often triggering more. The expert not only answers specific questions but can also draw attention to what has not been asked, further deepening the thought process and understandings.

Bridging differences

Experts can also be useful when there is extreme polarisation of opinion among participants. Here the expert brings broad experience of the situation, and often offers or generates innovative or creative—unexpected—perspectives.

Commissioned studies

Literature review

National, regional and international collection of published research is best assigned to a specialist—a person familiar with the subject area and able to use Internet and computer technologies.

Surveys

Surveys—which are principally a situation analysis—help participants focus on a realistic menu of options based on an authoritative position.

Mapping

Identifying who does what in a given subject area is best undertaken by a consultant, with tight terms of reference and dedicated "paid for" professional time.

Comparator visits

Best practices

Reading the theories on best practice is like having a recipe book for fine dining; a comparator visit is like going into the kitchen and watching a master chef at work—and actually "tasting" the best.

Centres of excellence

It is important that the places visited are truly outstanding and world leaders in their field. Their primacy is not founded on being very good at one thing; it requires all aspects of their operations to perform—separately and together—to an exceptional standard. Visiting them, and talking face- to-face with their leaders and managers, is the only way to fully understand what makes them so special.

Field visits

Broader perspective

The main purpose of field visits is to ensure all members of the task force understand what does and does not work in their own country. It gives them a perspective outside their own institutional setting, and gives them a hands-on experience of how others are tackling parallel issues.

Sounding board

Test driving the plan

Presenting a draft plan to independent and high-level decision makers

brings many benefits to the group dynamic as well as potentially improving the plan. It demonstrates teamwork, builds stakeholder confidence, and provides an opportunity to fix flaws and fine-tune details. The technique can also be used to put "insiders" in the hotseat—to help the leadership articulate its vision and perceived directions; to induct new leaders into the ethos of the organisation; to gain understanding of the staff mindset; to build confidence in the leadership; to rally support.

12 Other tools

> If you think there are thousands of ways to enable others to face challenges and produce results, think again. There are eight.

Leadership

We often blame 'leadership' when things go wrong and when groups are not working together. The problem with this rather simple and incomplete diagnosis is that it is not actionable, especially when people do not feel they have the capability to lead.

More constructively, there are three critical elements to leading individuals and groups from an undesirable present into a desired future, together. All have to do with language and framing:

- The practices of leading and managing—provide actionable language where none exists.
- The challenge model—frames a problem as a challenge that represents a tension between a "here" (current situation) and a "there" (desired outcome).
- Productive conversations—create a space in which it is safe to explore more deeply where the other person is coming from.

The practices of leading and managing

It is evident that effective public health leaders from around the world essentially engage in eight practices: four leading practices and four managing practices. The Results Model illustrates each of the practices while the Process Model shows how they interact to enable people to face challenges and produce results.

RESULTS MODEL

The practices of leading and managing

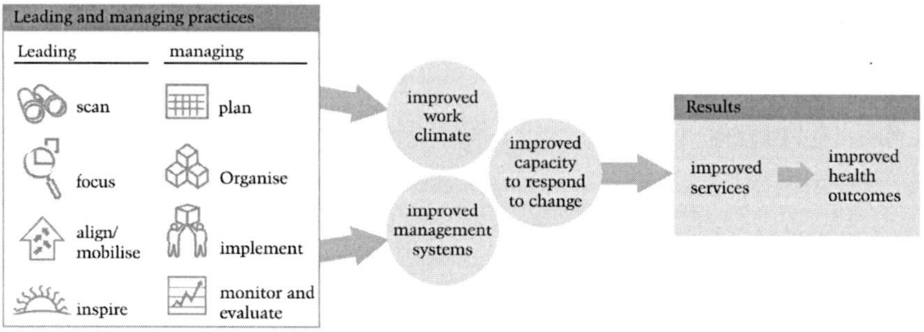

PROCESS MODEL

The process of leading and managing

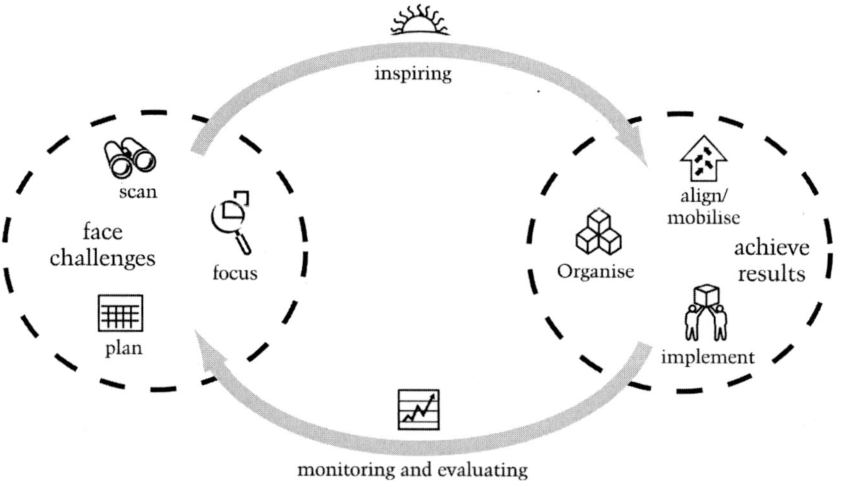

Note: Reproduced with permission from Management Sciences for Health (MSH).

The eight practices have been tested in hundreds of settings around the world—from Afghanistan to Zanzibar—among thousands of people at all levels. Each and every time they can identify those practices in the people they consider "managers who lead".

What does it mean to manage and lead? From the eight points the rational answer is: enabling others to face challenges and produce results (Management Sciences for Health, 2005).

Among other vital points, this debunks the popular notion if one person is a leader, the others must be followers. By the rational definition, any and all members of a group can be leaders, "enabling each other to face challenges and produce results".

- By twinning the practices that produce good leadership and those that produce good management as a kind of yin and yang of getting results, applied with a process of focused, disciplined and systematic thinking, individuals and groups are able to get from an undesirable present to a desired future—whatever it is!
- The practices of leading ensure we do not get stuck in the present, and the practices of managing ensure we do not overlook the importance of doing well in the present.

Although the research and testing of this approach has been mostly applied in the field of public health, it can easily be applied to any other field, including the very personal.

The Challenge model

People never develop leadership skills out of a book. Their ability grows as they take on challenges and succeed, and sometimes because they fail. This growth requires three essential elements:

- A compelling challenge that stretches current skills, knowledge and attitudes.
- Feedback and coaching to make sure lessons are learned and incorporated in new attempts at success.
- Supportive advice and encouragement when needed.

Before asking a team to focus on a challenge, a linguistic distinction between a "problem" and a "challenge" helps people transform from "victims" to "agents of change".

Participants can be asked to reflect on an accomplishment in their life of which they are very proud and (crucially) which was achieved in spite of considerable obstacles.

Without exception people can mention at least one example and the storytelling takes away any doubt that individuals can be highly effective if they want to be, even against overwhelming odds.

Problems are conditions we want other people to solve or take care of (i.e., 'we are poor, we have no money!') and which "they"—the government, the president, the donors—should do something about it. This is often said with considerable indignation, but with no solution or plan of action.

The Challenge Model is a simple and graphically self-teaching device that helps people to identify what to do next in a way that is fueled by:

- Aspirations rather than problems.
- The wishes for a better tomorrow rather than the problems of today.

By focusing on what is desired, a tension is set up between that desired future ("there") and the less-than-ideal present ("here"). This tension provides the energy to do the difficult work that comes from an honest and critical assessment of:

- What is keeping us stuck in the present and away from the results we seek to produce?

The model combines a series of planning methodologies but distinguishes itself from most by being aspiration-driven and single, short-term focused. This may seem counter-intuitive: there are many things to do and we should focus on the long term...but beware: many comprehensive planning processes leave people less confident and more overwhelmed. And nothing good comes from people who do not think they know enough (and need experts), or who do not know where to start, or who begin with the most difficult tasks and fail.

This in no way conflicts with the concepts of FPP, which takes on the most complex and comprehensive planning challenges of all. This is precisely why FPP uses incremental questions, to dismantle obstacles and build solutions...one step at a time.

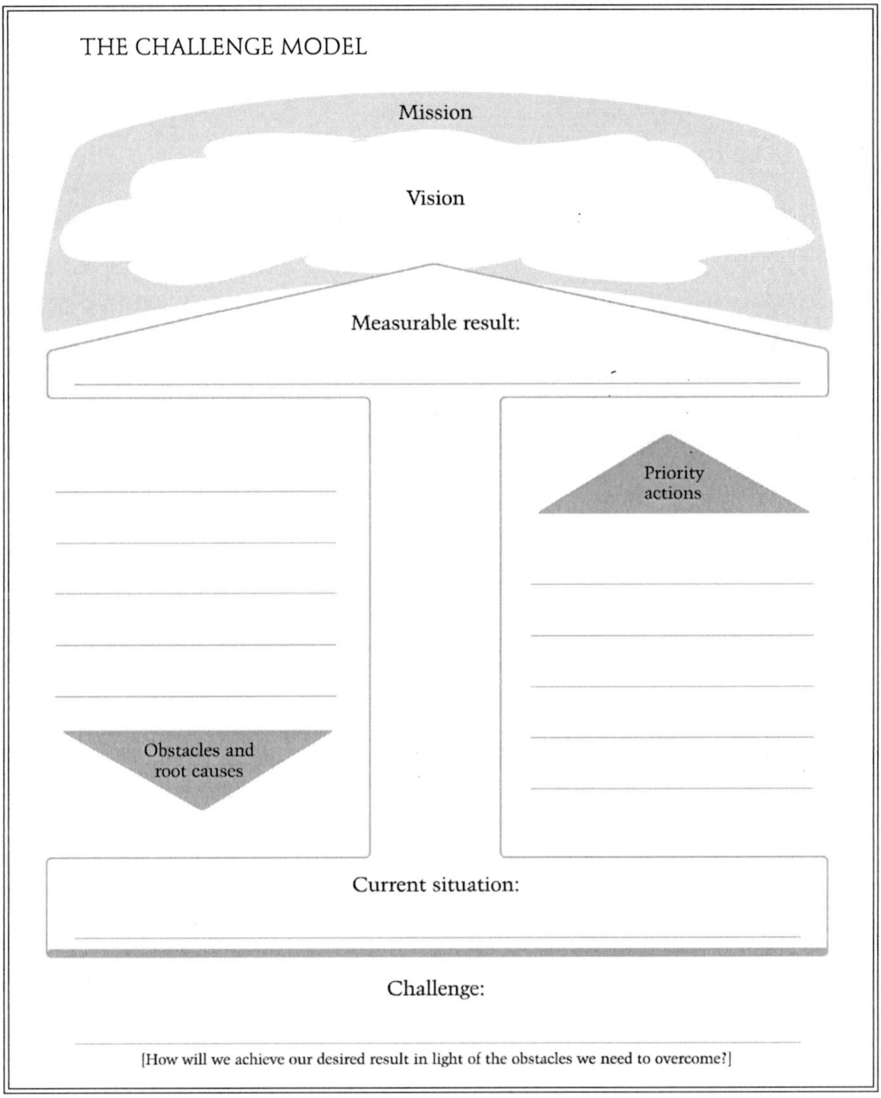

Note: Reproduced with permission from Management Sciences for Health (MSH).

In a nutshell, the Challenge Model, too, takes people through a simple questioning process:

1. Why are we here? To do what? (Mission)
2. If we did what we are supposed to do, what would we create in the far future? (Vision)

3. What would be one very compelling and important result to create in the next six months? (Smart result)
4. What is our current situation with respect to this one result? (Baseline)
5. Therefore, how do we achieve A given that we currently have B? (The framing of the challenge)
6. Why haven't we already accomplished this one result? (Root causes)
7. So what do we need to do to tackle these root causes? (Priority actions)
8. So who needs to do what by when to implement these priority actions? (Implementation plan)

Productive conversations

Groups or individuals often get stuck in polarised positions because of the illusion that one is right and the other is wrong. Both parties see a win-lose situation in any solution. And as neither party wishes to risk being the loser, the result is impasse.

There are certain patterns that can avoid this outcome and, instead, move the conversation to another level that produces goodwill, a better understanding of the other, and a willingness to search for new and creative solutions to overcome barriers to a shared vision.

In their eminently practical book on difficult conversations, Stone and colleagues remind us that in each broken-down conversation there are always three aspects: (Stone *et al.*, 1999)

- What happened, as experienced differently by each party.
- The feelings generated by what happened, and
- The impact of the experience on one's identity.

Most derailed conversations or stuck groups fail to acknowledge that:

- What happened depends on your viewpoint.
- There are always feelings involved, whether acknowledged or not, and
- Interpretations cannot be easily dissociated from our sense of self.

For example, if one version of a story, told by my opponent, describes my acts as uncaring or selfish, and I consider myself a very caring and selfless person, I am most likely to vehemently oppose that story. To make headway in a stand-off, the facilitator helps participants to acknowledge these three elements, presents differing viewpoints as valid, listens to the feelings, and recognises the underlying identity issues.

The Value Web

The Value Web is an international non-profit organisation based in Switzerland but operating globally. It offers ready-made, state-of-the-art models for exploiting the potential of "Group Genius"—a concept developed by futurists Matt and Gail Taylor (*www.thevalueweb.com*).

Though they do not subscribe to FPP's jargon-busting principles (they love the stuff!), they do capture the essence of diversity in collaborative planning, and above all recognise that a new world demands not just new actions but a whole new way of thinking and doing.

They drive this transformation of transformation with a modelling language which "explores challenges and relationships with new lenses"; a library of modules "to address and sequence design requirements" (such as Open Space Technology, World Café, Future Search and Scenario Planning); and ways of restructuring physical environments to reflect and optimise attitudes and performance.

They subscribe to the principles of GRASS (global, responsible, accountable, sustainable, stewardship) as fundamental and measurable values which every organisation must aspire to.

Pattern language

The "mood" of any individual or group varies—from happy to sad, positive to negative, energetic to weary, imaginative to dull, motivated to dejected, open-minded to bloody-minded.

It follows that one group on one day can be brilliant, while another group or another day can be dire. The difference in performance, if you are trying to get a team job done, is a major issue. Clearly, it is vital for facilitators—group by group, day by day and even hour by hour—to assess the mood, and:

- If it is negative, identify the cause and try to fix it.
- If it is positive, identify the cause and try to bottle it.

Many of the "talk-tuning" techniques and exercises in this manual are known-cause/known-remedy tools. The science of FPP is less equipped with techniques for diagnosing the cause in the first place, and relies heavily on the instincts and experience of the facilitator to spot a problem, to know what's wrong and why, and to choose the right fix.

The difficulty in devising a formula for this is that there are thousands of possible permutations of detail in each case. Diagnosis and remedy could at best be a mission almighty, and at worst a mission impossible. Indeed.

But while the reasons for swings in mood may be many (too many), they are not infinite. They can be counted. Even physically listed. And then clustered where differences stem from a common syndrome.

As a simplistic illustration, a group may be distressed by hard seats, or a cold room, or a stuffy room, or bright lights, or loud noise from an adjacent building site, or a lousy lunch, or cold coffee, or a smelly toilet... but all of these variables have a common (in this case obvious) denominator: physical discomfort.

Group mood is often affected by less tangible issues, more complex inter-relationships and deeper roots of attitude. But these, too, conform to a non-infinite and manageable number of syndromes...patterns.

By recognising and assembling these patterns, the number of permutations can be reduced to a few dozen. Few enough to give each one a name (for instant recognition and description) and to develop the best ready-made remedy which can be tested, learned and repeated (not hit-and-miss reinvented) whenever a problem arises.

That is what "pattern language" is about and seeks to do. The concept has been applied in diverse fields—indeed, it originated in architecture to find patterns in the relationship between designs (of whole towns, individual buildings, a single room and even a detail element like a door) and the intuitive human response to them.

Impacts on mood were researched, patterns were identified and named, so reliable, repeatable, ready-made solutions could be developed.

Recent work has applied the Pattern Language concept to group discussion, and has so far identified—and named, described and prescribed for—some three dozen patterns which can affect the mood and performance of a team.

A full description of this work (and many other management methods) is beyond the scope of this manual, but this brief mention serves to illustrate how FPP can harness a wide range of independent techniques to suit its own purposes (and principles), and to flag the fact that the toolbox is abrim with both established and new ideas. Facilitators are advised to be well read in adjacent fields.

Bottom line: The principles hold fast. The technology moves fast.

Section D

IN PRACTICE

13 Physical set-ups

Physical surroundings have a potent influence on how people think and act, so facilitators must take special care to make the working-room ambience and structure exactly right.

The working space

Standard VIPP uses the "campfire" set-up of chairs in a semi-circle—no tables, no lectern. Very pure, but not so practical where there is lots of writing to be done, or for "Zing" keyboards in a computerised system.

FPP by peer groups blends the importance of equality and informality with practicality and comfort. It uses tables with three to five people seated at the ends and on one side. Usually, these ensembles then form the nearest thing to a semi-circle that numbers and space allow, facing the pinboards/screen at the front (the communal fireplace).

While this represents best principle and best practice, clearly it cannot fit every location or situation, and facilitators (with the background reasons for the campfire principle in mind) must use their judgment to set up the arrangement that best suits circumstances and optimum group dynamics.

Whatever the final lay-out of chairs and tables, people who know each other in advance will tend to sit together—even strangers will tend to arrange themselves according to some perceived denominator, and by force of habit and social pressure, they will return to "their" seat at the start of each session.

A simple way to resolve this is to provide a seating plan at the beginning (a chart at the entrance door showing each individual's position) and/or

SETTING UP...

The room and lay-out encourages equality, informality and avoids the teacher-learner pitfall

place name cards at each place—carefully arranged to ensure a good mix of participants at each table.

Beware—"old hands" at seminars are adept at switching name cards around, so even if a master chart is not displayed it is a good idea for the facilitator to have a reference (or a very good memory). The facilitator may opt to maintain a pattern or "shuffle" the pack at regular intervals, whichever will deliver the desired group results.

Only a very small proportion of each FPP session is pure chat. In parallel with discussion, participants are constantly expressing thoughts visually—most often with coloured cards on pinboards, or the electronic equivalent using personal keyboards networked to a computerised master-screen. The board/screen is the focal point of almost every session.

And for anything visual, the first impact lies in appearance. Good FPP demands the right setting as well as strong content. This is an important consideration in selection of venue, room size and shape, furniture design, equipment, materials, and lay-out. Advance time and care to get this hardware right is more than advisable—it is necessary.

This is the environment—logistically, sensually and emotionally—where every word will be spoken, every idea will be hatched and shared, every problem sought and solved, every issue and opinion visualised and analysed, and every decision made and recorded. It needs to be very fit-for-purpose.

Ideally, the same venue meeting room will be booked and used for the entire planning process. The best settings are quiet and comfortable at a distance from the workplace of the members, such that attendance throughout the retreat is maximised and external disturbance minimised.

14 Know thy group

FPP by peers might ensure the group is homogeneous, but professionals generally have egos marked "fragile, handle with care". A bit like delicate crockery...or high explosives.

Working with professionals

Professionals are characteristically:

- Sensitive.
- Independent in their thinking.
- Proud and averse to embarrassment.
- Knowledgeable.
- Experienced.
- Opinionated.
- Set in behaviour patterns.
- Embedded in certain attitudes.
- Shaped by their cultural background.

As Paulo Freire puts it, adults:

- Do not give "wrong" answers.
- Learn only that which is beneficial to them; and
- Base their answers on experience and background.

SENSE AND SENSITIVITY...

is needed when dealing with adults, especially senior professionals who expect to get their own way

It follows that adults work together best when:

- They are involved and interested.
- The planning process is beneficial.
- They feel respected.
- They are challenged.
- They are comfortable.
- Planning activities are varied, and
- They have freedom.

In this context, it is really the power of the intelligent question which establishes the credibility and success of a facilitator, especially because it is only an outsider (who does not already know the answers) who can ask questions which are so basic as to be profound. Bold questions can get right to the heart of problems or solutions if the participants recognise that the facilitator is neutral and genuine.

There is a pitfall which the facilitator needs to be aware of: not infrequently, the champion/driver/chair or donor will try to influence the facilitator by providing biased information in considerable detail about various group members or about the complexities of the situation. Experience and the confidence which develops from working with groups will help the facilitator avoid or circumspectly manage this tendency.

The following "must" list for facilitators is important, but a 7-to-10 day training course for facilitators will provide the background and practice opportunities so essential for successful facilitation:

People profiles

Have an idea of who the participants are: their background and what they bring to the learning, planning and situational setting. This will normally be gathered while forming the Task Force with the Selection Board, through interaction with the champion/driver/chair or donor, and also through direct observation during sessions. Some of the games and exercises described in Chapter 9 can be especially revealing.

Key factors

Know the factors which can affect the planning or implementation (this is both a function of facilitation and the background of the facilitator). Often it is not possible for a training course to impart this except that, after each substantive session, the facilitator will hold a small, concise meeting with the two or three people in the group who he will rely upon to give guidance, answer tricky questions and such.

Rapport

Establish rapport through rules of respect, courtesy (even in times of tension, or with personalities who scarcely deserve it) and by inoffensively, avoiding answering certain questions which could jeopardise integrity and credibility.

Strategy

Proceed incrementally from the known (e.g. previous questions) to the unknown through a reasonably thought-out strategy, but recast a significant question in another way if the resulting answers and clusters are not helpful.

Preparation

Prepare well and be ready to troubleshoot—for example, get into the room to set up and organise thoughts one or two hours before participants arrive, which means getting there by 0700 hours in the morning if the session begins at 0800 or 0830 hours. Write out the questions on the cards in anticipation of the session. Review what happened at the last session; prepare to review filled boards by straightening out the cards, rewriting cluster headings and such.

Optimism

Expect the best out of participants but keep it light by injecting a joke or silly example from time to time.

Reflexes

Think fast (even the most experienced facilitator can never be on cruise control).

Respect

Exercise respect at all times, appreciate special circumstances, empathise with the participants, but keep to the code of conduct they set for themselves with a question like: What does the code require us to do in this case?

Neutrality

Be very careful not to force a consensus or decision where there is a conflict of ideas, perspectives, solution or choice. Let a contentious matter rest, give participants time to talk informally over lunch or tea, and then introduce a new thoughtful way to address the differences—for example through participants placing red dots (anonymously) on the solution they prefer. Again this requires preparation, setting the room up, cutting out the dots beforehand, carefully putting the instructions on a long card, always as a question: *Which of the two different problem statements do you feel best captures the issues?*

Control

Be firm when necessary. While the facilitator should never be rude, and should avoid any personal put-downs, s/he will need to play different roles at different stages to match the *forming, storming, norming* and *performing* patterns and properly regulate proceedings.

Remember always that the facilitator is expected to manage, co-ordinate, inspire and regulate the entire event. If things go wrong, it is only the facilitator who is responsible. That is why major meetings addressing complex subjects sometimes use two facilitators.

15 Planning a programme

FPP emphasises informality of style and adaptability of content, but there is a crucial difference between flexibility and chaos. Like even the most agile athlete, an FPP programme needs a strong skeleton to allow flowing and graceful movement.

The main steps

1. The project:
    - Initial cross-briefing between principals and facilitator.
2. The people:
    - Appointment and briefing of the Board of Selectors.
    - Selection of the Task Force.
3. The process:
    - The Task Force retreats—introductory and substantive sessions.
    - Between retreats there may be commissioned studies, field visits and comparator visits.
    - During retreats there may expert witness input sessions.
    - After retreats there will be production of reports on three levels (meeting, interim and final).
4. The product:
    - Drafting the Plan—appointment of an Editing Committee.
    - Task Force Review of the draft, and adjustments.

- Convening a Sounding Board forum.
- Finalising the Plan.

The project

The facilitator's first meetings are with the leaders of the organisation: the champions, the funders—the people who are "the principals".

In these meetings, the principals:

- Describe the organisation's background and supply supporting literature.
- Clarify the purpose of the project, and who they expect to participate.
- Indicate time and budget available for the exercise.
- May organise a meeting between the facilitator and the staff members and/or stakeholders.

In turn, the facilitator:

- Describes the FPP method and what it will require of the participants.
- Emphasises the democratic, open and transparent characteristics of the process.
- Explains the distinction between a facilitator and a conventional consultant.
- Emphasises that the process and its results belong to the organisation.
- Advises on the time and resources required.
- Explains that difficult moments will arise and affirms the organisation's commitment to working through these rather than giving up.
- Takes responsibility for designing the process.
- Explains how the Board of Selectors should be chosen.

The people

Once the Board of Selectors is in place, the first actual "facilitation" is with them and the principals, and it usually asks just one question: what are the personal/professional/status/age characteristics they would expect of a member of the task force. The answer might look something like this:

Personal	Professional	Status	Socio-cult.	Age
Honest	Med doctor	Head dept.	Religion	Over 60
Ethical	Academic	Agent of change	Ethnicity	45+
Motivated	Scientist	Leader	Politics	35+
Articulate	Recognised	Government	Gender	At least 28

In this example, the "age range" and "status" and "socio-cultural" clusters would need follow-up questions to clarify sufficient detail and to define the type and mix of persons the principals would like to see selected.

The facilitator then guides the selection process as described in Chapter 5.

Process preparation

The facilitator uses the briefing information to:

- State the objectives and expected outputs.
- Select and logically sequence the topics and the process strategy.
- Allocate each topic enough time.
- Select appropriate methods and materials, bearing in mind the objectives and number of participants.
- Develop an outline programme covering all the days or steps of the planning, evaluation or implementation process.

The initial design is just a guide; it will be revised during the actual planning to respond to unique situations which arise from all dynamic participatory processes. The facilitator must clearly explain the flexibility of the design to the organisation to avoid quibbles. The champion needs to recognise in advance that time slots will be negotiated and adjusted while topics may be added or revised—in whatever way best leads to the desired result.

Session preparation

The facilitator must also design each session appearing in the programme with the following details:

- Topic.
- Objective.
- Central question (follow-ups depend on the answers to the opener).
- Time slot.
- Methods to apply, including exercises, field visits, expert witnesses.
- Material requirements.
- Possible need for commissioned studies and/or comparator visits.

Timings

A mini FPP "event" may be completed in a single day, but more often will involve many retreats over several months. Typically, full programmes require 10 retreats of three days each, with the third day of each focused on "what the plan needs". Retreats can be held at intervals of about three weeks, each starting on a Thursday evening and concluding on a Saturday afternoon. Voluntary over-runs to Saturday evening, driven by sheer enthusiasm, are common.

There can be no fixed formula for time allocated to each topic or exercise within a retreat or session; this is very much a case-by-case issue and a key component of a facilitator's judgment and experience.

As a guiding principle, timing is a balance between "focus" and "progress".

1. Focus: Enough time to thoroughly air a subject, get to the heart of it, and establish a clear (though not always conclusive) position—but without digression. Some time limits help keep discussion relevant.
2. Progress: To maintain concentration and interest, and to get the whole job done within the time budget, FPP sessions need to "get on with it", to recognise when a debate has run its course, to avoid flat spots, to avoid belabouring extraneous detail. They should look to "move on" (to the next step) a little too soon rather than too late.

These principles apply constantly—to each part of each step of each topic.

Expert witness inputs can be prepared, conducted and debriefed in half a day. The witnesses usually join the group on arrival, sit through normal sessions and interact casually with the Task Force at meal breaks, and step up at their allocated point in the timetable.

Commisioned studies are conducted by others outside retreat time, but at least half-a-day is needed during a retreat for the researchers to present their report and answer questions.

Field visits are planned in session but conducted at the convenience of the team members assigned to the task, who also prepare their reports in their own time. If the reports constituted full descriptions, presentation could be inordinately long, so the facilitator restricts them to 15 minutes each, limited to answering two questions: What did you find surprising, profound or significant? The answer to that is followed by: What single insight to our planning task did your visit inspire?

Comparator visits are handled in a similar way, but as the locations visited are less familiar to the group, there is more interaction between teams reporting back and other members of the Task Force, so the debriefing can take the better part of a full day.

Reports require information to be captured as an ongoing part of every session, as a purely secretarial function. Efficient systems of capture and presentation (see Chapter 17) are necessary to minimise interference with session time.

The product

Towards the end of the programme, the facilitator and principals consult—based on observed individual performance—on who will be on an Editing Committee to draw together months of work into a coherent and formal plan.

Traditionally, the Editing Committee meets separately—for three days —before the final Task Force retreat. Although efficient capture systems make much of their task a selective cut-and-paste process, they need efficient desk-top publishing equipment and skills (through auxiliary technical support if necessary).

They present their draft to the Task Force at the final retreat, on Friday evening. The draft is fully discussed in a normal FPP plenary format through much of Saturday, with the drafters listening closely and taking notes, and speaking only when necessary to seek clarification of others' views. The facilitator orchestrates cards and clusters to assimilate key outcomes.

The Editing Committee revises the draft accordingly, and then the entire Task Force presents it to a Sounding Board comprising decision makers or people who must be sold the idea for it to progress positively. Again this

is conducted at a session using FPP principles and techniques to identify substantive issues, resolve them through working groups, and summarise considered revisions.

The final plan is then presented to the principals and is ready for "launch" at a subsequent partner consultation or stakeholder meeting.

Fund-raising strategy

All the institutions that have used FPP have depended on soft funding, so resource mobilisation is of fundamental importance.

Implementation strategy

The implementation strategy must be integral to the plan itself.

Start to finish

The facilitator must design every element of this process from start to finish, in advance, and meticulously prepare for every phase—of course to represent the highest professional standards (the future of an institution and all its stakeholders warrant no less) but also because...

...only if all the basics and back-ups are perfectly in place can a facilitator be steady enough and nimble enough to steer the project to an optimum course.

16 Phases of the session

A plan for reshaping the world from "how-do-you-do?" to "how-did-we-do?"

Once the cross-briefing between the principals and the facilitator is complete, the Board has been appointed and guided through selection of the Task Force, a start-to-finish timetable of Task Force retreats has been established, materials have been sourced and a venue has been chosen and equipped...

...there will typically be 10 Task Force retreats, phased in line with the forming, storming, norming and performing pattern.

Introductions

At the forming stage (usually the first day only), the emphasis is on participants getting to know each other and the technical and procedural systems of FPP, and fully understanding their role and purpose.

Positive attitudes

The storming stage (which develops on the second day and hopefully does not intrude too much on the third) focuses on changing attitudes from polarised positions towards teamwork, and at least flushes out and flushes away negative approaches. Participants also become completely familiar with the way FPP sessions, card systems etc., operate, so using them becomes second nature.

Hardcore information

Only when the group has started norming (day three or later) can information gathering be optimally planned—allowing half-a-day each to consider expert witness and field visits, and slightly longer for briefing a commissioned study or a comparator visit.

Final focus

The performing stage is where the most substantive group work gets done, earlier problems get fixed, comprehensive information flows in to a team in top gear, and the foundations of a plan are laid.

17 Charting the process

An FPP programme has introductory sessions, substantive sessions, evaluation and report. Each of these demands three crucial inputs from the facilitator: preparation, preparation and preparation.

Introductions

The first full Task Force session should be attended by the champion, who should make very short opening remarks to introduce the facilitator and to formally empower the stakeholders, both charging them with the responsibility and delegating to them the authority to decide the way forward for the organisation.

The champion then promptly hands over the process to the facilitator, both symbolically and physically.

Notwithstanding the imperatives of informality and flexibility, the first session should aim to:

- State the objectives of the event.
- Go through the mechanicals (cards, Zing) and the principles of participation.
- Explain why question-based FPP is employed.
- Allow participants to air their expectations and concerns.
- Reconcile those expectations and concerns with the objectives.
- Explain the methodology.
- Assign responsibilities to participants.
- Distribute resources to participants.

- Negotiate group norms such as a code of conduct.
- Agree on the (provisional) agenda.

Some or all the participants may be strangers to each other, and a "getting to know you" exercise can be a useful introduction (see Ice Breakers in Chapter 9).

Substantive sessions

In each session there is interaction between and among participants, with the facilitator, and there is information, time and space (indoor and outdoor). The emphasis changes as the group progresses through the forming, storming, norming and performing phases, but experience shows that all successful programmes—and each part of them—depend on:

Preparation

- Allocating the time for the process.
- Having a sufficient budget and making any/all payment systems clear.
- Having the right venue.
- Effectively arranging the room lay-out.
- Having resource materials ready.
- Carefully planning the introduction.
- Planning appropriate time for questions and answers.

Content delivery

- Sufficient coverage of topic.
- Logical sequencing of topics.

Attitude

- Readiness to learn from participants.
- Patience.
- Dedication to participatory question-based facilitation.

Approaches

- Use of real life examples.
- Proper use and management of space.
- Creativity.
- Flexibility.
- Recording (by facilitator/assistant) of important content.
- Co-option of experienced, knowledgeable and skilled participants into facilitation/assisting.

Communication skills

- Awareness and minimisation of distracting personal mannerisms.
- Talking *with* people not *at* people.
- Appropriate use of learning methods including games and exercises.
- Effective use of agreed spoken and written language.

Template for a retreat

Retreat plans are prepared by the facilitator, shared with the champion and outlined on cards for the group. This is how the first three-day programme might be charted (containing many principles which will apply to subsequent retreats).

1. **Opening:** The chair welcomes the participants, explains briefly why they are part of the group, and sets the purpose and goals. The facilitator is introduced and takes over the session.

2. **Introduction:** The facilitator has four immediate tasks:

First, to demonstrate leadership and give assurance:

- A presentation, using cards, of the ways in which human beings learn.

- A brief overview of the origins of participatory planning, including examples of successful processes which are familiar/relevant to the group (health examples for health professionals, etc.).

After each phase of this presentation, the group is encouraged to ask questions. The facilitator responds directly, writing the question on one card and the response on another, "naturally" demonstrating the card technique from the outset. At the end of this part, the card writing rules are formally presented, along with the six ways participatory processes are informed (see Chapter 5).

Second, the facilitator would have measured the mood of the group and now selects the most suitable method of introductions.

- This could be self introductions, through a central question with a creative twist: "What three personal characteristics of yours are most relevant to this group?" Each participant would write them on three separate cards and then be asked to stand and present.
- If members are not known to each other, the facilitator might pair them off to interview each other and then introduce their partner using the same question or some variation. The facilitator could participate in this, or fit in a brief professional/personal sketch as response to any questions from participants.

Third, the facilitator begins a card session with the question: "What are your two/three greatest expectations of this planning process?" The immediate collection and clustering is followed by the question: "What are your fears regarding the goals/purpose of the planning process?" This question should be completely "open" and the facilitator should not give examples of possible or appropriate responses but allow participants to think for themselves—generating a range of topics, including fears about the participatory process, the ambitious goals, the composition of the group or the limited time frame, for example—and establishing the ethos of the process. The collection of expectations and fears gives the facilitator and the chair information which might need to be addressed immediately, or used later on in the cycle for evaluation purposes, depending on what is put on the cards.

Fourth, the facilitator manages a short session in which the code of conduct is established, sometimes through a card collection or possibly through brainstorming (which is more efficient) or mind-mapping using the laptop computer and a projector. Ample time is devoted, as this process is important to group formation and self-regulation. The code empowers the facilitator and the chair or secretariat to implement what the group decides, but does not railroad their decisions. It covers such points as substitutions, absenteeism, late arrivals, early departures, mobile telephone protocol, listing of names of attendance, conflict of interest, starting and finishing times and whatever else the members, chair or facilitator believe is essential. The code must be developed by the group itself, triggered by questions from the facilitator if necessary.

The opening and introductory session usually takes about two hours to get a group of 12-20 up to speed; it is often undertaken on the evening of arrival (6.00 pm to 8.00 pm) for a residential meeting, or in the early morning (8.30 am to 10.30 am tea break).

3. **Substantive sessions:** The first substantive session has three components.

It begins with a central question of great significance to both the subject and the process. Significant and broad questions are best suited, allowing exploration of the big picture. There are two strategies the facilitator can launch—one problem-based (what's wrong?) and the other challenge-based (what would be ideal?).

Problem Questions	**Challenge Questions**
What are the three most significant problems facing delivery of health services?	What would be the essential or ideal characteristics for an effective health delivery service?
What are the two most debilitating/inhibiting/constraining aspects of effectiveness for the new highly qualified professional entering your institution?	What aspects of your institution would attract/empower a new highly trained professional who you wanted to work in your institution today?

Either set will generate significant responses, allow ample scope for heated debate and yet enable broad (not specific) agreement.

The facilitator moderates by ensuring inclusiveness and keeping the focus on ideas, not decisions. These types of questions will consume a couple of hours each and ensure participants have the opportunity to express themselves, exert their personality and display their knowledge. Importantly, the facilitator gets a chance to gauge the group dynamics, which are vital to the next session...where the participants will break out of plenary into working groups of 4 or 5 people each.

The next step is to take the boards containing clusters of either "problems" or "visions" and separate them into distinct divisions. The facilitator then forms an appropriate number of small working groups and assigns each the task of developing the plenary results into a fully articulated one- or two-page statement.

Each group will have the same assignment but a different "problem" or "vision" to work with. This work ideally begins immediately after the lunch break. The facilitator selects group members based on the dynamics observed during the plenary, distributing people to optimally develop the group dynamics and test the development of team performance.

The facilitator monitors group work in terms of how and who they select as their chair, secretary and presenter and then in terms of how they work. Ample time is allowed, provided the working groups demonstrate sufficient and sustained energy. Once the task is nearing completion, and before members become bored, the facilitator indicates a wrap-up deadline, giving 15 to 30 minutes for groups to conclude.

The final component of this process is for each group to report back to plenary. Here, the facilitator guides groups to not defend their work, but to offer clarification on the how and why of their results. It is important that each group has ample time to present; usually 30 minutes is sufficient. Each group is obliged to record on cards the comments and suggestions made by the plenary and, when back in group mode, is then given 30 minutes to discuss and implement the revisions they feel are necessary or reasonable.

The end of this revision period would be a normal and appropriate point at which to end the day's work.

The experienced facilitator employs a variety of techniques to give each session an edge, a sense of significance, a fresh way of tackling an issue. This keeps the participants engaged, attentive and productive. It prevents them from "predicting" and thus pre-meditating. These techniques include: walkabout, buzz groups, card collection and clustering, one-dot evaluations for prioritisation, plenary, group work, expert witnesses, exercises, problem solving, model creation and field visits, comparators and commissioned research (as described elsewhere in this book).

Materials

Materials required (for conventional card technique, as opposed to Zing etc.) for 20 participants:

- Six moveable pinboards.
- 200 white, 100 yellow, 100 blue, 100 green, 100 pink small rectangular cards.

- 20 large rectangular cards in pink, 20 white and 20 green.
- 300 stick pins.
- Pair of scissors.
- Stapler.
- 30 ball-point pens.
- 30 black or blue felt-tip marker pens.
- 5 red, 5 blue and 5 green felt-tip marker pens.
- Two rolls of masking tape.
- One long ruler.
- Four flip charts with stands.
- One packet of adhesive colour dots.
- One laptop computer, one printer, one digital camera and one LCD projector.
- One ream of A4 typing paper.
- Four extension cords for participants to plug in their laptop computers.

GETTING READY...

Successful FPP demands the right venue, the right set-up, the right materials and...preparation, preparation, preparation

Parallel operations

Evaluation

Evaluation is beneficial both during and at the end of every event, focusing on different aspects and using different methods. Some key areas are:

- Extent to which objectives have been achieved.
- What participants liked most or least in the content and process.
- Realisation of expectations and reduction of fears.
- The appropriateness of methods used.
- Effectiveness of the facilitator role.
- Duration of the event.
- Level of participation.
- Overall usefulness.
- Specific achievements, planned and unplanned.
- Overall organisation and logistics e.g., accommodation, food, venue, time management, adequacy of learning resources used, transportation and any other aspect which participants may consider important.

Programmes can use established rating methods or invent new ones. Whatever the method used, the evaluation needs to:

- Indicate exactly what is to be evaluated.
- Be participatory.
- Be transparent (there is no other or behind-the-scenes monitoring going on).
- Be simple and clear (for ease of administration and synthesis of results).
- Be creative (fun to do, interesting to collate, graphic impact).

- Be open and honest.
- Produce instant results; and
- Capture information quantitatively and qualitatively.

Some popular methods of evaluation are (see also Chapter 9):

- Rating scores: Usually on a scale of 0-5 against each aspect and marked on a board using adhesive labels and marker pens. Each participant takes time to mark his or her ratings without influence.
- Flash words: A one word/phrase expression about the event. The participants and facilitator sit in a circle and the facilitator asks a very direct question to the plenary. Each person gives a personal opinion in a very short (even one-word) statement, going around the circle one by one. Discussion is not allowed as the flash is going on. The facilitator captures sentiments expressed on cards and pins them on a board.
- Pre-test and post-test: To gauge what changes have occurred in participants' knowledge, skills and attitude as a result of the event.
- Self critiques: Participants assess themselves against a set criterion.
- Daily committee: Collects views and suggestions from other participants for feedback to improve the event by the day. A different committee of two or three participants is nominated each day for the task. (This is the most appropriate for events lasting five or more days).
- Memo board: Participants post their comments on a board, at any time on any aspect. The facilitator monitors the board to determine any action required, and discusses its contents at the beginning of each day.
- Written questionnaire: Which participants fill in individually, to measure aspects deemed important.
- Mood metre: A visualised chart with faces expressing different emotions against which participants mark their level of satisfaction at the end of each day's work. It helps to gauge the atmosphere of the workshop. The facilitator marks the middle point for each day and later draws a line joining them to show the 'ups' and 'downs' of the group.

Report preparation

FPP generates two types of report:

- **Meeting reports:** essential internal records for the Task Force itself
  - as a basic professional diligence and contingency.
  - for motivation (seeing the record is satisfying and encouraging).
  - for personal review (further checks and thinking on certain issues).
  - as reference (reminder) material for the team that writes the plan.

  Meeting reports also give the Task Force something tangible to share with funders/principals if an interim track of activity/progress is demanded. They reassure stakeholders that the process was thorough.

- The plan itself (or prospectus or proposal)—which is the core purpose and formal conclusion of the whole process.

Both are products of the participants. The facilitator does not add content or comment, but s/he does ensure material is "captured" in-session and guides the production process.

Meeting reports

Meeting reports do not need to be time-consuming syntheses or analyses; they do not need to prove anything by copious volume; they do not need to be works of art. They are, literally, a record of what was done—at the end of each retreat and, cumulatively, at the end of the event. That generally means:

- A photograph of every completed pinboard (or the equivalent transcription/print-out from computerised systems).
- Photographs of people/activity (exercises, buzz groups, plenary etc.).

- Any other pertinent material used (graphics, analysis, flow charts, evaluation results and such) either noted or reproduced as appropriate.

...all neatly arranged and labelled in accordance with the sequence and title of each session. The facilitator must ensure—either personally or by assignment to assistants and/or TF members—that the material is captured in real time (hour by hour, day by day), selectively collated as a mandatory exercise, and that the skills and equipment for rapid reproduction are available.

In any reporting, speed is important—to demonstrate professionalism, to capture the essence while memory is still fresh, while enthusiasm is still high, and to ensure time efficiency. A benchmark is production of reports within 48 hours. Reputations get dented if it takes longer than that.

REPORTING...

It is important to capture key moments at each stage of the process

Problems associated with photo reports include:

- Photographs are no good if the cards and other materials were illegibly written—if the facilitator did not insist on participants following card-writing rules.
- Poor photographs (less likely with digital) that will lose quality when photocopied.
- Poor photocopying facilities, which will again compromise quality of the final product.
- Sense of incompleteness because the rich discussions that go on during the event are not captured. And photographs—which must be meaningful, even to the outsider—only capture representative moments.

The format is not perfect, but it is realistically meaningful, useful, and quick.

The Plan

The ingredients of the Plan start to take shape in the "norming" and "performing" stages of an FPP programme. Issues are resolved, strategies are agreed and priorities are set intrinsically. As described, Working Groups within the TF are also assigned to drill down on details, present their drafts to plenary, and revise according to feedback.

In the closing stages of the programme, entire retreat(s) are focussed on this process, so before the end every element of the Plan has already been drafted and peer-reviewed and each "section" exists as a distinct document.

In parallel, the facilitator (often in consultation with the champion/ principals) has assessed the intellectual and technical acumen of each participant and is well able to select and assign an "editorial team" to put all those elements together in the shape of a professional Strategic Plan, with a logical sequence and unified style.

Remember, the people doing this are already working as a high-performance team; each and all have intimate and common knowledge of the issues and details; meeting reports are an existing reminder; democracy is already built-in to the source material, and it remains intrinsic in the "editing" process.

The final Plan is further presented to plenary and ideally subjected to "Sounding Board" scrutiny and experienced suggestions, usually at the final retreat.

The editorial team adjusts in accordance with those inputs. The final product handed to the champion/funders/principals is a true, thorough and highly-refined "result" of the FPP programme.

Of course, the Plan still may have its detractors and opponents; but to an extent which is unrivalled by any other planning process. It is likely to have the general acceptance, the positive buy-in and the active support of all legitimate stakeholders.

This is the very essence of FPP; its distinctive super-merit! The plan it delivers is made by the stakeholders. FPP gives them a thoroughly digested and mutual understanding of all the issues, from all angles. FPP builds their mind-set and team spirit to a level of high performance. The editorial team is not just from this specialist group; it is the best possible mix of the most capable members of this group.

The process of drawing up a final plan, by these people in these contexts, is dramatically more relevant, informed, effective, balanced, co-operative and fired with enthusiasm than traditional forms of brainstorming, collation and drafting.

It remains the Principal's prerogative to "polish" the final product, using specialist editing and design to fine tune the visual quality of a document aimed at a specific audience (e.g., donors, shareholders, policy makers). But they interfere with the integrity of the plan's fundamental proposals—its real intent—at their peril.

To counter any remaining risk of "outside interference" with the plan's principles and implementation, the Principals (the organisation for whom the Plan is made) can appoint "trustees" to monitor and defend its integrity. Members of the original Selection Board, or TF members themselves, are both well qualified and well disposed to do that.

Section E

DELVING DEEPER

18 Freqently asked questions

1. How long does this FPP process take? Normally between six months and one year, depending on the frequency of meetings, duration of meetings and complexity of the circumstances.

2. How much does FPP cost? Cost depends on the number of participants, the duration and number of meetings, whether residential or not, where comparator institutions are located and the extent of detail required in the plan/proposal/prospectus. As a perspective, the innovations at Makerere planning grant was $78,000 while the REACH-Policy Initiative involving three countries, sounding board meetings with 10 international members and launch with donors and a good quality published prospectus, had a total cost of $130,000. The College of Health Sciences planning grant was more expensive at $178,000 with a large group over a one-year planning cycle involving eight residential weekend retreats, comparator visits to Asia, Europe, Middle East and North America.

3. Do planning team members receive any payment for their work? Yes, an honorarium is usually provided of between $50 and $150 per day. But in all the cases presented in this book, except one, this honorarium was paid only for time spent outside of normal office hours. The rational is that professionals are paid by their employer, groups have consistently discouraged "sitting" fees and emphasised membership in their professional and individual capacities, with fees not based on consultancy rates but given as an expression of good will and to encourage attendance. Groups always develop a code of conduct and in all cases except one, participants were not given the honorarium unless they spent the entire time working in the group, e.g. only one FPP process has paid the honorarium for appearances shorter than 6 hours out of an 8 hour day.

4. How can I train to become an FPP facilitator? There are no routinely offered courses, but you can contact the author, Cole P. Dodge, for announcements at places such as the Makerere Institute of Social Research (MISR), UNICEF and Bangladesh Rural Advancement Committee (BRAC) where occasional courses are offered. There is also an international network of Visualisation in Participatory Programmes (VIPP) which already offers annual training and advanced training, and has FPP training under discussion.

5. What agencies or donors will fund these long-term FPP planning processes? The donors who have funded them include: Rockefeller Foundation, Canada's IDRC, Ford Foundation, Carnegie Corporation of New York, and many of the bilateral donors as well as World Food Programme and UNICEF (usually in specific programme areas which they initiate). However, all donors are interested in sustainable and significant planning processes because implementation is made so much easier. Too many funders engage consultants in the planning of their programmes with minimal involvement of local professionals (except as sub-contractors or consultants) which leads to problems at the implementation phase. Therefore, it is incumbent upon the policy makers, managers, planners and leaders who read this book to convince their partners in development about FPP as the best way to go about planning for new institutions, or for transformation of existing ones, and that it is cost-effective in the long run.

6. What is the optimal time frame for an FPP process? Some FPP processes can be scheduled over as little as two or three meetings, often a preparatory planning meeting of three to four days, leading to a week-long residential meeting and followed by a sounding board meeting of two days, and finally a stakeholders launch. In Asia, where planning is readily recognised as an integral part of institutional processes, it is common to use FPP in a single week-long process, especially when participants are drawn from the same institution or divisions of a large organisation. In Africa weekend retreats are more readily accepted, especially when participants are drawn from senior levels and diverse institutions. The rhythm involves commencing after the work week on Friday evening and running up to a late lunch on Sunday, with evening sessions closing around 10 p.m. and beginning at 8 or 8:30 in the mornings. Six such retreats would probably be minimum while 8 to 10 would be optimal. In countries where residential meetings would not be culturally appropriate, other options can be explored.

7. How many people should there be in a planning Task Force? The lowest number that gives sufficient diversity—small groups often work more efficiently and this would include groups of between 6 and 10. More commonly there needs to be at least a dozen, up to a maximum of 20 where a national institution is being created or transformed. The ideal number from a facilitator's point of view is 14 to 16.

8. Does the Task Force appoint a chair? No, not the Task Force. However, principals appoint a representative as the institution's project "driver", who may act as the chair. Where the donor gives a grant to an institution, the institution appoints the chair. S/he is often the head of the institution or head of a planning department, and is a person with a burning desire to create or transform to meet emerging needs, challenges or address big problems or opportunities. These leaders are the ones who have embraced FPP in the first place. They have to supervise the secretariat to make sure that communication flows and that administrative and financial tasks are done. They also form a partnership with the facilitator to ensure that the process works. (see Chapter 3)

EXECUTIVE STATUS...

Whoever sits in the chair, the job is to marshal the conduct of meetings, not to boss the ideas or decisions

9. How can we contact an FPP facilitator if we want to move forward? Experienced professional facilitators are not abundant, but this book offers several sources of reference—the author, the publishers, and the case study projects.

10. Who will own the final plan/proposal/prospectus? The final product is owned professionally by the members of the FPP Task Force and commercially by whoever commissioned them, but there is often an institutional home which officially receives, approves and implements. Sometimes a new institution is created with various interim arrangements.

11. Is there a budget template which would help us write an FPP proposal for funding? There are many ways to present a budget and therefore it is best to follow the guidelines of the funder or develop your own using these key questions:

- Who (and how many resource people) will you invite to join the Task Force and how much of an honorarium will you provide?
- Will you tackle the FPP planning process in several short weekend retreats or in three or four longer sessions?
- Will you use your own conference room or take the group to a residential setting?
- Who will pay the facilitator and how much will that cost?
- Will you pay for transport? Are there any air tickets involved?
- Will you visit comparators; if so which countries are they most likely to be in?
- Will you do field visits for two days and how much travel will this involve?
- Will you base your budget on costs or per diem entitlements?
- What will the small secretariat consist of and will this be within an existing institution or will people be hired part time to service the FPP process?
- Will you use cards and board or zing or MindManager to capture the proceedings?

12. Can you double the meeting times and thus reduce the number of meetings? Yes, meetings can be of any duration. If you can get the commitment of members during the busy work week and if they agree not to ask for payment or consultancy fees for their time then any combination of timing is possible. The reason weekend retreats evolved was to assure attendance; remember you are dealing with very senior people and therefore the normal practice of paying sitting allowances will not be proper for an FPP process.

TIME AND EMOTION STUDIES...

Longer sessions are not an effective way to reduce the time or improve the quality of the FPP process

13. If we cut down on the number of participants can we reduce the budget? Of course; however, small elite committees of very senior professionals have been appointed and they work very efficiently only to encounter disappointment when it comes to approval and/or implementation...because there was insufficient stakeholder involvement. People no longer accept hierarchy of the powerful, prestigious and privileged when it comes to planning for a nationally important institution.

14. How many comparators, field visits and expert witnesses do you need for a successful FPP? All members of an FPP process need to go on a field visit in their own country. These are frequently within the capital city and sometimes nearby so the cost is relatively modest. In some cases, Task Force members team up for field visits, which enhances team unity and improves dynamics. Expert witnesses tend to be very senior people who are busy, so identify twice as many as the number you think you need, simply because the "no-show" rate is at least 50 per cent. Generally, four to six expert witnesses will suffice. While it is desirable that members all visit a comparator, air tickets are expensive. The budget is rarely if ever sufficient for full fare air tickets, nor can government or even UN per diems be given to everyone. Usually, and successfully, a few are selected from the group and manage on a flat sum. At the beginning of FPP everyone imagines that the planning grant contains "entitlements" because that is what they are used to from donors and governments. However, as the "storming" phase transforms into the "norming and performing" they recognise that FPP is entirely their own and there is no donor organising, paying or determining the outcome, nor topping up the budget.

15. What venue is best for FPP retreats—a local or more remote location? This varies from country to country and within countries from institution to institution, depending on the reliability of the members and discipline. Having said that, most planning meetings work best if they are a little way out of town, so Naivasha and Kiambu in Kenya, which are 70 and 20 km respectively, Entebbe or Jinja in Uganda which are 35 and 80 km respectively and either Rajendrapur (40 km) or Savar (30 km) in Bangladesh are the sorts of distance which have worked best.

REMOTE CONTROL...

FPP sessions should be held where all participants can be fully focussed, without distractions or interruptions

16. What happens if some members do not turn up regularly for meetings?. This disrupts the process of group work and team-building as well as the flow of incremental questions. Therefore, at the beginning of each FPP process, the facilitator asks the group how they would like to govern and regulate themselves. Time-keeping and attendance are in that list. The group develops its own terms of reference and code of conduct. Usually, a member who misses two consecutive meetings loses membership. Deputies and substitutes are not permitted. Participants are appointed as individuals, and not as representatives of institutions.

17. Who takes the minutes and records the proceedings? The "minutes" are really just a record of the boards (which themselves represent the issue, discussion and outcome) digitally photographed and chronologically downloaded onto a laptop. The facilitator requires an assistant who can manage the computer, attend to funds, draft letters and such. It is really very simple and straightforward. "Action shots" are also taken and are edited by the facilitator into a normal "word" document ... the report is ready for distribution soon after the close of the meeting (printed in black and white, burned onto a CD Rom or flash drive, and then sent as an attachment to an e-mail).

18. Should meetings be held in the same venue or is it okay to rotate to new locations? It is very important that the facilitator help select the venue, because of the unique room set-up, need for rotation between plenary and small working groups, late night and early morning access to working space, security of the computer, printer and digital camera. The facilitator should do an evaluation at the end of the first meeting with the first questions specifically related to the venue. If the group respond favourably, it is far better to stick with the venue, important for group formation and harmonious working, comfort and predictability (the hotel staff grow to understand the needs of the FPP process). If Task Force members are spread across a large country, rotating locations may be considered more equitable.

MERRY-GO-ROUND...

Regular changes of venue may be necessary in exceptional circumstances, but are not generally recommended

19. What is the optimum interval between retreats? Three weeks is ideal, four weeks works fine, but anything longer runs the risk of participants not recalling what happened at the last meeting, requiring a longer review session at the outset of each meeting.

20. What is the ideal composition of a Task Force? A reasonable gender balance (never less than 30 per cent women and optimally closer to 50 per cent) at least 15 per cent drawn from the young professionals category (probably not senior, but identified as leaders with exceptional track records and good prospects) and whatever else is deemed important by the Task Force selectors. It is important to remember that Task Force members are chosen on the basis of their potential contributions, and not as representatives of their respective institutions.

21. Should members be given a certificate for participating in an FPP event? This should not be expected as necessary or important, given the seniority of the participants. When FPP or VIPP training is undertaken, "graduates" receive a certificate appropriate to the level of qualification attained.

22. What is the dynamic of converting the planning team into an implementation or management team? While this is a good question to be put to the Task Force just before they are adjourned, do read Chapter 12 on the difference between leadership and management. Generally the Task Force hands over a plan, which is then put into action by the institution's own implementation systems.

23. Should there be a directed or managed attempt to maintain the relations and connections at the end of an FPP process? No, the bonding and networking have already been realised and any connections which persist will do so on their own merits. However, as the plan is implemented the original Task Force may be useful in an annual review.

NETWORKING...
The people get together to make a plan, not the other way around

24. What should happen to the final plan/proposal or prospectus? This needs to be addressed at the outset by the principals. Usually the results should be professionally packaged and distributed purposefully to the decision makers and wider stakeholder group.

25. Is there a choice of facilitation techniques if there is a constraint on money or time or management for planning? There are no shortcuts in the effective FPP process, and cost cuts will mostly depend on the willingness of participants to do the work in lower budget conditions.

COST CUTTING...

The venue budget may vary, but there should be no shortcuts in time or content

19 The makings of a facilitator

> The FPP concept can and will be applied in every sphere of life, everywhere. In the face of universal demand for accountability, transparency and stakeholder involvement, it will be the go-to method for solving problems and making plans.
>
> Facilitators will be in great demand...if they are good enough.

Proficiency level

Effective FPP facilitation needs more than technical know-how. It is an advanced skill which requires professional training from the outset, a further period of understudy to achieve basic competence, and many years of practical experience to attain mastery.

This book gives a grounding on "what" the FPP process involves. That is a very long way from knowing "how" to do it; and knowing how is yet another quantum leap from practical experience.

People already qualified and practiced in other training disciplines might have a head start (in talents, confidence and some practical skills)...but even they still have a long way to go.

For a key feature of FPP is that it is not like conventional methods. It is not just a new twist on the many ways of team-building and group planning that have been the staple of past decades. It is an entirely different approach.

Certainly, this book and professional training in FPP will give the seasoned leader/facilitator of conventional management courses some new insights and techniques; and these might be usefully applied piecemeal. Indeed, FPP concepts are so intrinsically positive that they can be helpful in almost any context. But a full FPP event to meet a complex challenge requires the complete package to be delivered in very particular combination and detail.

Consider: in a training course or conventional group planning exercise, even mediocre tuition/leadership can still get the job done with tangible outcomes. Even if the teaching is mediocre and mistakes are made, good students still acquire skills and pass tests; strategic plans and log- frames are still generated. The knowledge exists, pre-packaged, and simply has to be delivered. Teacher knows. Learners listen.

In FPP, the Task Force is not a "class" acquiring set knowledge from an expert, nor a group under orders to deliver a pre-ordained product. It is a collection of wholly independent individuals representing polarised positions and with no inclination nor obligation whatsoever to reconcile their differences or conform to authority. And yet they must, to a greater extent than in any conventional training or planning course, be forged into a high-performance team to devise an effective solution to a complex problem. Their job is to work together to reveal undiscovered knowledge—the "unknown"—and use it to create a unique product that is so mutually understood and agreed that all are proud to own it. This transformation must be achieved without a whiff of hierarchy.

The person who facilitates in that context needs a different mindset, a different skill-set, true leadership and a high level of technical proficiency. In sum, second-rate FPP facilitation is likely to get a second-rate result... and may get no result at all.

Special aptitudes

An FPP facilitator needs all the attributes and skills of a conventional trainer...plus a lot more. The FPP process demands even stricter adherence to concept principles but at the same time it must be conducted more flexibly, more democratically, and in a much wider variety of contexts. This requires an extra dimension of techniques, a rare mix of presence and diplomacy, and reflexes that are both fast and precise.

The benchmarks of innate acumen, confident personality, leadership character and comprehensive know-how are high. The conversion rate of trainee to expert is low.

However, for those with the talent—and the determination to learn and then master the special skills—FPP facilitation offers a rewarding career path at a senior consultancy level, in a pioneering field that is likely to generate global demand in every sector and institutional context. It has serious potential in the evidence-policy arena.

Training

The foundations

The essence of FPP is visualisation, participation, and facilitation. Its cardinals are incremental (blue-sky) questions and teamwork. Those are the ingredients which enable it to frequently achieve results that other processes cannot.

Each of these ingredients has its own set of concepts, principles and techniques. The facilitator must be a master of all parts of all of them.

To put the scale of that learning in perspective, just one aspect of visualisation is the card system. The facilitator needs to give the Task Force that tool in less than 10 minutes and use it effectively throughout. To do so, s/he needs to be proficient in more than 100 distinct pieces of practical skill. Some of those pieces are intuitive; others are not. Some are nuts-and-bolts hardware; others are subtle but vital variations of style, mood and timing.

In turn, cards are but one of several tools and techniques of visualisation that FPP uses, ranging from print and photography to LCD projections and high-tech computer programmes. FPP facilitators must not only know of these, but choose just the right one at just the right time and use it in just the right way...with ease, so the tool does not detract from the thought. Facilitators must also budget them, arrange them, and manage them.

It gets tougher; some degrees of skill are "unteachable." For example, questions are central to the process and their content and quality can be all-important. Very subtle nuances can make the difference between complete confusion, or total silence, or a magical moment of understanding, agreement and progress.

Facilitators can be taught and must know the difference between many different types of question—convergent, divergent, probing, leading, rhetorical, simple, compound, multiple-choice, productive, reproductive, and their do's and don'ts. But the choice of question, its vocabulary, its phrasing, and which of several follow-up options should be used...these are matters of timing and touch that come only through practical experience.

The training process

There are as yet no established training or certification systems in place for FPP facilitation. These will come. Meanwhile, champion institutions have engaged master facilitators to conduct pilot training exercises, to establish both the optimum format and the levels of proficiency attainable in given time frames.

In line with FPP's own principles of "learning by doing", the most effective format has been found to be the FPP process itself—visualisation, participation and facilitation, driven almost entirely by questions and conducted through teamwork. In this way, participants learn the principles, the process and the practice at the same time.

At least five days of intensive orientation, instruction and participatory process are required to cover the foundations, in sufficient detail that the most talented students would be able to co-facilitate an FPP event.

While those with less natural ability would need longer to embed the learning and refine their practice (or indeed recognise that expert facilitation is probably not their career path), all who undertake such a course will gain useful insights and additional skills.

Course content

Outline

This single chapter is clearly not a draft syllabus nor a curriculum, and it is certainly not the beginning of a training manual.

The reason becomes clear through a simple list of the main content headings of the five-day (20 sessions) foundation course—bearing in mind that for each of these headings there are dozens of sub-sets, and for each of those there are several dozen detailed skills; the whole amounts to several thousand distinct elements.

Five-day template

A five-day course should give participants:

- A clear understanding of the origins, concepts and principles of FPP, sufficient to know where its application is suitable, the role of the facilitator, and to uphold the integrity of FPP's process and purpose.
- Knowledge of the process and its methods, techniques, tools and practice sufficient to effectively co-facilitate every aspect of an FPP event.

The foundations of an FPP event include:

- **Selecting the Task Force**: balanced, representative, committed, capable...often chosen in a political minefield.
- **Arranging an FPP event**: budgets, timetable, venue, facilities, equipment, logistics...up to 10 retreats, spanning a year.
- **Facilitation**: role, principles and required skills...in everything from human nature and pins and pens to computer software.
- **Participation**: leadership, time and logistics management, learning techniques, group dynamics, teamwork.
- **Visualisation:** concepts and tools; generating, capturing and depicting ideas.
- **Interrogation**: incremental questions...that are relevant, clear, inspire ideas, and take the team step-by-step to success.
- **Evaluation:** assessing ideas, priorities and practicalities, assuring champions and donors, keeping focus on targets.
- **Compilation:** documenting progressive outcomes, filling information gaps, tapping case, specialists and best practice, legal issues.

- **Results**: delivery of an agreed plan, testing it with experts and stakeholders, refining, and driving implementation.

The facilitator's role in an FPP event includes:

Preliminaries

- Liaison with the event champion and sponsor/donor on the design requirements, challenges, objectives and expected outcomes of the event.
- Guiding selection of elders/chiefs, and steering their work in setting up a balanced and representative Task Force.
- Preparing a time and cost budget for all elements of the entire event and negotiating its confirmation.
- Agreeing on the facilitation team, role and mandate, and the source and composition of secretariat support.
- Selecting and inspecting venue(s), and supervising organisation of all facilities, equipment, transport, accommodation and other logistical arrangements.
- Assuring correct invitation/pre-briefing of Task Force members.
- Drawing up a draft schedule, and advance preparation of methods and materials.
- Physically setting up working area(s) to meet all process requirements—physical, logistical and atmospheric.

Process

- Managing hand-over of the Task Force from the champion to the facilitator (transfer from hierarchy to participatory) including confirmation of commitment to process and purpose.
- Engaging the Task Force, and introducing core principles (visualisation, participation, facilitation, centrality of questions, etc.) and procedures (technical operations, sources of information,

capture of ideas, methods, etc.) using step-by-step "learning by doing" techniques.

- Establishing agreed codes of conduct, management of breach or dissent, peacemaking, peacekeeping.
- And, covering all that cascades in a single sentence: Progressively maximising the performance of the Task Force through every aspect of the programme.

To maximise performance, the facilitator must know how to astutely manage:

- Group dynamics—building confidence and enthusiasm, tapping synergy, integrating cliques, learning curves, "safe harbour" discussions, and contingencies of last resort.
- Individual personalities—adults, professionals, building respect and rapport, resolving conflicts, allowing flair to thrive in a team context.
- Active, balanced participation—democracy and energy, creativity, group mood, games and exercises, co-ordination, focus.
- Team building through forming, storming, norming and performing phases—focus and progress, patience, integrity.
- Visualisation methods—cards, MindManager, Zing and more, planning ambitious objectives...not inhibited by imposed terms-of-reference goals.
- Capture and recording methods—integrity and efficiency, photography, desktop publishing, secretariat.
- Plenary and break-out sessions—advance preparations, group sizes, brainstorming, deeper analysis, space and logistics, pacing.
- Games and exercises—judicious choices, purpose, challenge levels, individual sensitivities.
- External information sources—time and cost constraints, protocols, political awareness, building constituencies.

The facilitator must be expert in the selection and conduct of core methods including:

- Incremental questions—types, phrasing, reproductivity.
- Establishing problem statements—to focus the work.
- Generating, capturing and analysing ideas.
- Commissioned studies—external research to fill information gaps.
- Field visits—local trips to broaden perspectives.
- Comparator visits—trips to see international best practice.
- Expert witness—interviewing external specialists.
- Sounding boards/reference groups—experienced outsiders.
- Stakeholder forum—feedback on the near-final draft.

Training can (and must) tick those lists and all that cascades from each of them in concept, principle, rule, method, technique and tool. Knowledge and technical proficiency can be refined through co-facilitation practice and astute observation. To that, only the facilitator him/herself can add the final essential ingredients: talent and wisdom.

References/selective bibliography

Bergdall, T.D. (1993). *Methods for Active Participation*. Nairobi: Oxford University Press.

Blackburn, J. and J. Holland (1997). *Who Changes? Institutionalizing Participation*. London: IT Publication.

Chambers, R. (1997). *Whose Reality Counts? Putting the First Last*. London: Intermediate Technology Publications.

———. (2002). *Participatory Workshops: A Sourcebook of 21 Sets of Ideas and Activities*. London: Earthscan.

Chowdhury, M. (2007). "A Bangladeshi Approach", *Bulletin of the World Health Organization* 85(12), December.

College of Health Sciences (2002). *Prospectus*. Makerere University Faculty of Medicine (*Max-Plan.com*), February.

de Savigny, D., H. Kasale, C. Mbuya and G. Reid (2004). *Fixing Health Systems*. IDRC.

Dodge, C.P., N.B. Musisi and M. Okumba (2002). *Question Based Facilitated Participatory Planning.* MISR.

Dodge, C.P., N. Sewankambo and E. Kanyesigye (2003). "Participatory Planning for the Transformation of the Faculty of Medicine into a College of Health Sciences", *African Health Sciences* 3(2), August.

Dodge, C.P. and P. Wiebe (1985). *Crisis in Uganda—The Breakdown of Health Services*. Pergamom Press.

East African Community (2006). *Reach Policy Initiative Prospectus*. EAC.

Fals-Borda, O. and M.A. Rahman (1991). *Action and Knowledge: Breaking the Monopoly with Participatory Research.* New York: Apex Press.

Freire, P. (1970). *Pedagogy of the Oppressed*. New York: The Seabury Press.

Friedman, J. (1992). *Empowerment: The Politics of Alternative Development*. Cambridge Mass: Blackwell.

Hamilton, D. and U. Gaertner (1991). *Goal Oriented Project Planning (GOPP): An Introduction to the Methodology*. UNDP Office for Project Services.

I@mak.com (2001). "Application Guidelines for Funds", Makerere University, May.

Kaner, S., L. Lin, C. Toldi, S. Fisk and D. Berger (1999). *Facilitator's Guide to Participatory Decision-Making*. Brussels: Institute of Cultural affairs.

Klabert, K., S. Einhard and G.S. Walter (1992). *Winning Group Results*. Hamburg: Windmahle.

Mamdani, M. (2007). *Scholars in the Marketplace*. Fountain Press.

Management Sciences for Health (2005). *Managers Who Lead: A Handbook for Improving Health Services*. Cambridge: MSH.

McKee, N. (1993). *Visualisation in Participatory Programmes*. UNICEF.

McKee, N., E. Manoncourt, C.S. Yoon and R. Carnegie (2000). *Involving People Evolving Behaviour*. Penang: Southbound.

Miruka, O. (n.d.). *Visualization in Participatory Programme: Application in Cultural Orientation for Relief Workers*. Sudan.

Musisi, N.B. and C.P. Dodge (2002). *Transformation in Uganda*. MISR.

Newstrom, J. and E. Scannell (1998). *The Big Book of Team Building Games*. New York: McGraw-Hill.

Rasmussen, P.E. (1998). *Participatory Approaches to Development*. Danish Association for International Co-operation.

Salas, M.A., J.T. Herman, N. McKee and N. Shahzadi (2006). *Visualisation in Participatory Programmes (VIPP): How to Facilitate and Visualize Participatory Group Processes*. Penang: Southbound.

Schnelle, E. (1997). "The Metaplan Method: Communication Tools for Planning & Learning Groups", in *Meteplan Series* No.7. Quickborn.

Stone, D., B. Patton and S. Heen (1999). *Difficult Conversations. How to Discuss What Matters Most*. New York: Penguin Books.

Strategic Plan (2001). *2002–2005*. Makerere University, Planning Development Department, November.

Tuckman, B.W. (1965). "Developmental Sequence in Small Groups", *Psychological Bulletin* 63: 384-399. The article was reprinted in *Group Facilitation: A Research and Applications Journal* 3, Spring 2001.

UNICEF (1996). *Education for Conflict Resolution: A Training Manual*. New York and Geneva.

———. (1998). *Games and Exercises: A Manual for Facilitation and Trainers Involved in Participatory Group Events*. New York.

Vaughn, P. *et al.* (2005). *Scoping and Design Missions for a Collaborative Health Research Capacity Strengthening Programme in Kenya and Malawi*. DFID Health Resource Center.

Wiebe, P.D. and C.P. Dodge (1987). *Beyond Crisis—Development Issues in Uganda*. MISR and African Studies Association.